"Dr. Fatemi's book has provided a landmark contribution in the field, illustrating how films can be potentially valuable in psychotherapeutic settings. Clinicians as well as researchers will benefit from the comprehensive, pertinent literature and creative concepts in the book and learn about how movies can pertain to psychoanalysis, relationships and development, mindfulness, and learning modules. Implementing films in psychotherapy offers invaluable avenues in the therapeutic process, and provides unique and diverse points of entry in mental health care."

—**Bruce Kirkcaldy, PhD, FBPsS**, *director, International Center for the Study of Occupational and Mental Health, Düsseldorf, Germany*

"In this milestone book, Sayyed Mohsen Fatemi takes us on an existentially informed cinematic journey. We are guided through a series of reflections about how films can foster mindfulness; a 'psychology of possibility', for readers suffering from a myriad of conditions. Fatemi shows how great cinema can provide people who have over-identified with parts of themselves to open to a larger and more enlivened outlook. I highly recommend this book for anyone who works with, suffers from, and inquires into a deeper dimension of living."

—**Kirk Schneider, PhD**, *adjunct faculty, Saybrook University and Teachers College, Columbia University, USA; author* of The Polarized Mind, Awakening to Awe *and* Horror and the Holy: Wisdom-teachings of the Monster Tale

"Dr. Sayyed Mohsen Fatemi details how multifarious layers of a film have the potential to elucidate the possibility of describing, explaining, analyzing, interpreting and deciphering the dynamics of the psyche. He offers a broad assortment of film therapy strategies and techniques that may be used with a wide range of clients and mental health issues, including the use of film in psychoanalysis, mindfulness training, relationship enhancement, and social and emotional development."

—**Edward Kruk, MSW, PhD**, *president, International Council on Shared Parenting; associate professor, School of Social Work, The University of British Columbia, Canada*

Film Therapy

Unlike any book on the market, *Film Therapy* introduces a new paradigm in exploring the subtexts of movies and their potential therapeutic dimensions. The book illuminates how feature films can entail psychological components that can facilitate the therapeutic process. By elaborating the key concepts of each film and their psychological and psychotherapeutic discussions, this book provides a demonstration of films' practical applications in a therapeutic setting, opening a new world for understanding and exploring the dynamics of films in human interaction. The book powerfully delineates the rarely discussed role of films in psychological realms and argues how films can be educationally inspiring for therapists, psychologists, and educators.

Sayyed Mohsen Fatemi, PhD, completed his postdoctoral studies in psychology at Harvard University where he has also served as teaching fellow, associate, and fellow. He has practiced psychotherapy for over a decade and has been a recipient of the Ellen Langer International Mindfulness Award.

Film Therapy
Practical Applications in a
Psychotherapeutic Context

Sayyed Mohsen Fatemi, PhD

NEW YORK AND LONDON

Cover image: © Getty Images

First published 2022
by Routledge
605 Third Avenue, New York, NY 10158

and by Routledge
4 Park Square, Milton Park, Abingdon, Oxon OX14 4RN

Routledge is an imprint of the Taylor & Francis Group, an informa business

© 2022 Taylor & Francis

The right of Sayyed Mohsen Fatemi to be identified as author of this work has been asserted by him in accordance with sections 77 and 78 of the Copyright, Designs and Patents Act 1988.

All rights reserved. No part of this book may be reprinted or reproduced or utilised in any form or by any electronic, mechanical, or other means, now known or hereafter invented, including photocopying and recording, or in any information storage or retrieval system, without permission in writing from the publishers.

Trademark notice: Product or corporate names may be trademarks or registered trademarks and are used only for identification and explanation without intent to infringe.

Library of Congress Cataloging-in-Publication Data
Names: Fatemi, Mohsen Sayyed, author.
Title: Film therapy : practical applications in a psychotherapeutic context / Mohsen Sayyed Fatemi.
Description: New York, NY : Routledge, 2022. |
Includes bibliographical references and index. |
Identifiers: LCCN 2021032774 (print) | LCCN 2021032775 (ebook) |
ISBN 9781138338814 (hardback) | ISBN 9781138338852 (paperback) |
ISBN 9780429441431 (ebook)
Subjects: LCSH: Motion pictures in psychotherapy. |
Motion pictures--Psychological aspects.
Classification: LCC RC489.M654 F47 2022 (print) |
LCC RC489.M654 (ebook) | DDC 616.89/1656--dc23/eng/20211103
LC record available at https://lccn.loc.gov/2021032774
LC ebook record available at https://lccn.loc.gov/2021032775

ISBN: 978-1-138-33881-4 (hbk)
ISBN: 978-1-138-33885-2 (pbk)
ISBN: 978-0-429-44143-1 (ebk)

DOI: 10.4324/9780429441431

Typeset in Times New Roman
by Taylor & Francis Books

Contents

	List of figures	viii
	About the Author	ix
	Preface	x
1	Films as Learning Modules	1
2	Films and Psychoanalysis	10
3	Films and Mindfulness	17
4	Why and How Films Can Be Therapeutic	35
5	Films and Relationships	43
6	Films and Understanding	49
7	Films and Development	56
8	Films and Emotion	61
9	Films and Global Wisdom	69
10	Films, Signs, and Symbols	75
11	Film Therapy in Action	89
12	Films, Politics, and Education	95
13	Film and Poetry	114
	Bibliography	124
	Index	140

Figures

A Beautiful Mind (2001)	6
The Birds (1963)	13
Guess Who's Coming to Dinner (1967)	18
I Am a Fugitive From a Chain Gang (1932)	32
A Beautiful Mind (2001)	35
Compulsion (1959)	37
Forest Gump (1994)	38
I Am a Fugitive From the Chain Gang (1932)	39
Scarlet Street (1945)	44
The Graduate (1967)	47
Bajrangi Bhaijaan (2015)	54
I Confess (1953)	56
Cast Away (2000)	61
Dead Poets Society (1989)	65
Dead Poets Society (1989)	65
Titanic (1997)	70
I Am a Fugitive From a Chain Gang (1932)	92
Life of Pi (2012)	93
Rocky (1976)	96
The Life of Emile Zola (1937)	112

About the Author

Sayyed Mohsen Fatemi, PhD, completed his postdoctoral studies in the Department of Psychology at Harvard University where he has also served as a teaching fellow, an associate, and a fellow. He is a frequently published author and has been the keynote speaker of numerous international conferences. In addition to teaching at Harvard, he has taught for the Department of Psychology at the University of British Columbia; Western Washington University; University of Massachusetts in Boston; University of Toronto; York University, Canada; Endicott College; and Boston Graduate School of Psychoanalysis. Dr. Fatemi is also an adjunct faculty member in the Graduate Program in Psychology in the Department of Psychology at York University, Canada.

His publications appear in journals such as APA's *Journal of Theoretical and Philosophical Psychology* and *International Journal of Clinical and Experimental Hypnosis* and have been published by Springer, Wiley, Templeton Press, Routledge, Cambridge University Press, Oxford University Press, Lexington Publications, Palgrave Macmillan, and the American Psychiatric Association.

He brings mindfulness into his psychological and therapeutic interventions and has run training and coaching programs for clinicians, practitioners, and corporate people in North America and overseas. He has been practicing psychotherapy for more than a decade.

Dr. Fatemi is a recipient of the Ellen Langer International Mindfulness Award and is an active member of APA with numerous presentations at APA annual meetings. Furthermore, Dr. Fatemi has served as an associate professor of psychology and the chair of the Desk of North America at Ferdowsi University of Mashhad, one of the top five universities in Iran.

Preface

Therapy occurs in a relationship and impacts a relationship. It is meant to change, improve, or help manage a relationship. Different therapeutic schools of thought apply different techniques and interventions to facilitate and implement therapy in action. Their given praxis and emphasis over the choice of specific methods are embedded within their theoretically accepted postulations and axioms.

This book argues that along with sundry methods of treatments and available treatment plans, films can open a new avenue for putting into effect the therapeutic process. This would suggest that specific films can be considered to develop a treatment plan. The plan may involve watching the entire movie and/or underlying special features that may contribute to the therapeutic goals.

There have been numerous studies on films and their impacts (see, for instance, Janicke et al. 2017; Oatley & Djikic, 2018; Oatley et al., 2018; Tan, 2018). Multifarious layers of a film have the potential to elucidate the possibility of describing, explaining, analyzing, interpreting, and deciphering the dynamics of the psyche. Wedding and Niemiec (2014) have discussed tens of movies and their psychological themes, psychological categories, and psychological implications. Other studies have addressed the psychoanalytical dimensions of films and their expansive platform with their unconscious repertoire of meanings (see, for instance, Diamond, 2016; Sabbadini, 2014).

Attention to the use of films in therapy has been emerging in recent years (see, for instance, Bierman et al., 2003; Dermer and Hutchings, 2000; McCullough & Osborn, 2004). Other studies have indicated that both therapists and clients have found films to be a great tool to help and facilitate the therapeutic process (see, for instance, Lampropoulos et al., 2004). Films have also been examined and discussed in detail in connection with their psychological impacts in various areas (see, for instance, Niemiec & Wedding, 2006; Wedding & Niemiec, 2003, 2014).

Films offer an in-depth and opulently rich panoply of psychological themes and psychology in action where one can observe the multifaceted and complex human interaction in a wide variety of contexts. All senses are displayed and put into effect with their extensions. The saliently

Preface xi

conspicuous sense in films unfolds its manifold expansions in the visual sense followed by the auditory sense and other accompanying senses. The human entity, its quiddity, and its features are all exhibited in a film with the director's concentration on some aspects—namely, magnifying one or some dimensions while minimizing or marginalizing some others.

A viewer may be entrenched in a film so much so that the borders between real and unreal may be dissipated. Films can delineate the interplay of human emotions and cognitions and their entanglement in different realms of life. They may sometimes express straightforward allusion to situational, such as *The Hurricane* (1999), *I am a Fugitive From a Chain Gang* (1932), *The Shawshank Redemption* (1994), *Hacksaw Ridge* (2016), and *Silence* (2016).

Movies may also narrate human suffering on a personal and individual level: *Gaslight* (1944), a classic movie, and *Unsane* (2018), *Wonder* (2017), *Cyberbully* (2011), all modern movies, may instantiate how human beings are victimized, belittled, downgraded, humiliated, and demolished by the actions of others.

There may be a display of values and their power in constructing and giving direction to one's life in movies as movies such as *I Confess* (1953), *A Man for All Seasons* (1966), *The Third Man* (1949), and *Life Is Beautiful* (1997) might entail.

It may be safe to say that movies may have the potential to represent, misrepresent, distort, explicate, and illustrate human life and its quality. The representation may sometimes be embedded within the human encounter with the bitterness of experiences and their phenomenological bearing. Movies such as *Scarlet Street* (1945) from the classic list and *American Beauty* (1999) may be examined in this regard.

Nafas (2016) and *A Separation* (2011) may be enlisted among contemporary Iranian movies that presage the celebration of devotion and values, love and perseverance, emotional and spiritual growth, and leap beyond the ordinary. *When the Moon Was Full* (2019) exemplifies another international film in the Persian language that demonstrates the façade and configuration of extremism.

Film therapy focuses on the complex relationship between humans and the film environment. In film therapy, one may acknowledge the significance of stories and narratives in constructing our lives. Ellen Langer and I (Fatemi & Langer, 2018) have discussed the therapeutic implications of stories in shaping who we are and who we choose to be. Movies present lenses through which psychological analyses can be made on the strength of different relationships.

Films may be examined in terms of their aesthetics where levels of attractiveness, beauty, and suggestions are associated with provocativeness. The spiral impact of visual and audio senses and prompts may strengthen the sensation and perception of beauty in a Gestalt-oriented context.

In exploring the aesthetics of films, Münsterberg indicated that "the photoplay tells us the human story by overcoming the form of the outer

xii *Preface*

world namely space, time, and causality, and by adjusting the events in the form of the inner world, namely attention, memory, imagination, and emotion" (2002, p. 129).

The dialectics of the inner world and the outer world manifest differently in emergent mental, emotional, physical, and behavioral responses. Mind and films are ineluctably tied to one another, and they both entail an aesthetic quality. In the mind, they do not copy reality.

In discussing Münsterberg's analysis of films, Carroll has suggested that

> for in the matter of film depth and motion, the psychologists tell us we add something to the visual array, whereas with the deep close-up, the selecting is something that is done for us. That is, the mental process-attention that Munsterberg discusses with the respect to the close-up is, roughly speaking, in the film not in us. A similar shift in direction occurs in the rest of Munsterberg's account of cinematic articulations.
>
> (1988, p. 491).

In film therapy, films may be taken as texts in their broadest sense in that they convey meanings. Texts can be subjected to analysis, deconstruction, decoding, and interpretation. The same holds for movies as they can be the subject matter of numerous analytical viewpoints and they can be conceptually and practically explored in terms of their ingredients, their discourse, their impact, their potential, and actual levels of demonstrations. Levels of text analysis in films can vary depending on the approach, the perspective, and the methodology.

It is important to note that different schools of therapy may approach films based on their postulations and premises. A therapist focusing on psychoanalysis, for example, may view a film in a way that complies with his or her axioms and principles and may highlight or focus on parts and pieces that make sense in his or her structural approach. A therapist with an interest in cognitive behavioral therapy may lead the discussions and the choice of a specific film in a manner that ultimately helps the client to identify his or her dysfunctional thinking. On the other hand, a therapist with a tilt toward existentialism may bring into light specific components of a film that would move in line with existentialism as a system of psychotherapy and a system of philosophy.

A word of caution needs to be stipulated here that the choice of the film, the discussions, the process of asking questions, the feedback, the assignments and the analysis, and the focus in each session need to be taken into consideration based on each client's case; their education; their age; their cultural, ethnic, family, social, and political contexts; their ability and competencies in cognitive and emotional levels; their history; their relationship status; and any other variables and factors that may have an impact on processing the selected films.

Films may be subjected to broad analysis or microanalysis based on the intention, the focus, and the objective of the therapy. One may therefore

Preface xiii

address how a given film may be examined in light of its potential for presenting a philosophical perspective on life and one may sharpen one's focus on a sentence or an effect in a film. The selectivity would sit together by the extrapolation, argumentations, extractions, and conclusions created between the therapist and client. The dialogical relationship of client and therapist would enhance the quality of the discussions and the richness of the conclusions. This would also strengthen the interplay of both intellectual and emotional flux of the conversations.

Listening to clients, their views, and their feedback on the film may also bring about helpful moments of empathy, support, and understanding. The world of imagination is an invaluable source for creativity, novelty, hope, well-being, health, and wellness. The potential to see the realm of possibilities, the domain of dreams, the spectrum of visualizations would bring hope and illumination. Films are innately interconnected to the world of imagination, creativity, and novelty. They can open the infinite possibilities of the human soul and the delicacies of human characters while portraying and elucidating the complexities of psychological dynamics. Films may associatively conjure up the entertaining impact, which first and foremost is tied to their nature of creation. Films can also present their exquisiteness in demonstrating other potential effects in the sphere of therapy. Films embody the multidimensionality of humanness in their presentations, ranging from bitterness and brutality to love and affection, from animalistic behaviors to acts of divinity, from the mundane engagements of routinized habits to the interplay of the unconscious eruptions.

In films, we may see the newness of thoughts, the change of fates, the glamor of playfulness, and the depiction of social and individual malaise. Films may operate as a great source of inspiration, instruction, and enlightenment. They may walk us through the ups and downs of life and the meandering of feelings, affects, and emotions while passing through the avenues of cognitions and thoughts. Films may explicate the power of perception, the strength of imagination, and the force of attitudes. They may mirror our anxieties, our worries, our compulsions, and our stalemates.

Films may be psychologically examined in terms of their impact on viewers and their effect on spectators, and they can be explored in connection with their creators: the intentionality and the psychological dynamics of film directors, screenwriters, and film producers. Correspondingly, the characters in the films may be the subject of psychological analysis and may be studied in terms of their affective, cognitive, emotional, and behavioral implications. The analysis may go through the seemingly perceptible signs of sensibility within the film configuration or may delve into the structural levels of meaning including the unconscious layers.

Along with the multidimensionality of films' potential in highlighting sundry demonstrations of artistic, philosophical, psychological, and cultural manifestations of human life, films may be taken into consideration to employ, implement, and bring about therapeutic goals. The therapeutic

xiv *Preface*

use of films presupposes an in-depth understanding of the psychological nature of films and their immensely powerful medium and mode of communication that can entail the quintessential array of human dynamics.

The essence of films may open cynosures of effectiveness in transmitting numerous applications in the human world. Therapeutically speaking, they can be employed to point out the range of helpfulness in providing a ground for facilitating therapeutic applications. They may be discussed in terms of their overall theme for facilitating the importance of a social–cultural topic as they may delineate the calamity of being afflicted with a psychological disorder. They may indicate the paths to overcoming obstacles and impediments while substantiating the rigor of steadfastness and positive emotions. Films are unlimitedly potentiated to give rise to horizons of thoughtfulness, mindfulness, and creativity.

They can be discussed in terms of their power for modeling as they can be considered for their signification for highlighting emergent issues. Films can be creatively examined and analyzed for different therapeutic goals. Therapists need to have a keen perception of the underlying psychological and theoretical foundations of films as tools and they need to pay attention to the delicacy of the contexts where films are introduced or discussed. The receptiveness of clients' contexts and sensitivity toward clients' backgrounds in a film may play pivotal roles in the success of using films as a therapeutic tool.

Film therapy may serve as an effective psychological tool for emotional awareness, emotional management, mindfulness, and emotional creativity. Furthermore, films may be discussed, analyzed, and employed in the proper contexts with a focus on couple therapy, family therapy, and psychological disorders. The protocols for using films in any of the abovementioned areas need to be tailored to clients' needs, preparation, and assessments. The interactive process of dialogues between therapists and clients requires a climate of empathy, understanding, rapport, and cultural sensitivity. The discussions need to be systematically arranged by the topics, their orders, their implications, and their thematic analysis.

The following chapters discuss and demonstrate how films can bring about a new horizon for psychotherapy.

1 Films as Learning Modules

Learning is defined as a change in behavior that may occur in different contexts and through different media. Traditional modes of learning are often associated with the use of books, whereas the new ways of learning have brought about attention toward newer forms of media such as technologically based forums.

Numerous studies indicate that films have served as a significant educational tool for learning in various spheres, including medicine, counseling, education, nursing, and psychology (see, for instance, Alexander, 1995; Alexander & Waxman, 2000; Fleming et al., 1990; Karlinsky, 2003; Nelson, 2002; Raingruber, 2003; Toman & Rak, 2000; Wedding et al., 2010).

Films have been proven to be of great value in offering hope, perspective management, problem solving, relationship management, positive thinking, inspiration, resourcefulness, empathy, well-being, role-modeling, inner journey for self-empowerment, self-efficacy, and self-awareness and understanding the role of values in one's life (see, for instance, Berg-Cross et al., 1990; Hesley & Hesley, 1998; Schulenberg, 2003; Wedding & Niemiec, 2003).

Some studies, albeit with small groups, have indicated how films may operate as a helpful therapeutic tool for the treatment of depression, self-esteem enhancement, prosocial behavior, coping strategies, emotional awareness, emotional expressiveness, and empathy (Bierman et al., 2003; Marsick, 2010; Powell & Newgent, 2010).

Wedding and Niemiec (2014) argued that watching films with a positive psychological theme can positively impact personal growth, well-being, self-improvement, societal growth, emotional development, and prosocial behaviors.

Long before the studies mentioned above on psychological aspects of films, Bruner (1966) indicated that people's thinking styles might be influenced by their exposed images. According to Bruner, "Man is seen to grow by the processes of internalizing the ways of acting, imagining, and symbolizing that 'exist' in his culture, ways that amplify his powers" (1966, p. 320).

DOI: 10.4324/9780429441431-1

2 Films as Learning Modules

Likewise, Stein et al.'s experiments (1979) corroborated the relationship between exposure to films and learning new skills, new cognitive tools, and thinking styles.

Berg-Cross et al. (1990) were the first who used the term *cinema therapy*. Cinema therapy was meant as a form of therapy in which a therapist selects films with a focus on his or her client's areas of concern. The client, in cinema therapy, was encouraged to watch specific films alone or with specified others.

Films can provide an effective tool for learning the connection between the content of the films and the client's personal life as they can open up or present issues that may not be openly discussed in the therapeutic meetings. Some clients may have difficulty touching upon issues directly and explicitly, and films may help them explore them more safely and securely.

Learning may be pedagogically associated with schooling and forums that develop a formal medium for implementing learning. Nonetheless, the most entertaining activities, including playing, may unfold their rich potential to offer and illuminate various learning levels.

Not surprising, films may be employed as an effective and creative instrument to conduct learning, evoke thinking, promote intellectual engagement, and discuss emotional connectedness.

Learning can be addressed to an individual, a group, a family, or a couple. Movies may also provide opportunities for discussing emotions, feelings, thoughts, and behaviors. Emotions are represented in films in both verbal and nonverbal forms. Positive emotions, including happiness, joy, and exhilaration, or negative emotions, such as sadness, regret, and anger, are displayed in a wide variety of contexts. Emotions may be triggered through evocative description or provocative elucidation.

Notice the following lines from the movie *Titanic* (1997) and their demonstration of emotions:

ROSE: A woman's heart is a deep ocean of secrets.

ROSE: It was the ship of dreams to everyone else. To me, it was a slave ship, taking me back to America in chains. Outwardly, I was everything a well brought up girl should be. Inside, I was screaming.

Titanic (1997) may be discussed in terms of its polysemic messages and their pedagogical implications. On the one hand, the movie can be explored in connection with the taken-for-granted assumptions, including the invincibility of the ship; those aboard the ship take it for granted that the ship will never sink. It is indefatigably capable of navigating the ocean. In line with similar assumptions, those who see the signs of fire in *Titanic* from afar cannot believe that the ship has been set on fire; they describe it as a sign of celebration. On the other hand, when it comes to saving the passengers, the rich are given priority. The movie depicts the class struggle and the domineering discourse of power, even in the hardest human conditions.

The movie celebrates the panacea of love in disseminating the walls of differences, divisions, rifts, and discord. It demonstrates how love conquers seemingly insurmountable problems and gives rise to the apex of glory in dealing with human encumbrances.

Titanic (1997) offers a potpourri of emotional power in motivating human behavior. The movie delineates how anxiety and tension may espouse a narrow scope of attention. The movie may suggest scenes and dialogues where the limbic system's activation takes precedence over human behavior. The movie may serve as a rich resource for displaying emotional expressiveness, emotional manifestations, and contagion of emotions.

Therapists may explain different perspectives of an experience while evoking different aspects of the film. On one level, one may operate from a participant's perspective and experience the participant's experience. In the illustration of the movie's love story, Rose and Jack are deeply involved in the participation model. They are engaged in participating in their exchange of love, both verbally and nonverbally.

On another level, one may operate from an observer-participant perspective where one observes their participation. When coming from an observer-participant perspective, the interplay of observation and participation will develop a dialectics of understanding the interdependence of action and agency. One may see how their action may be embedded within their scope of the agency. Observation will enhance the possibility of inner agency in implementing their action.

The third level takes place where one does not participate and merely plays the role of an observer. Therapists may invite a client to watch the film and see how different parts of the film may provide different levels of experience. By evoking different experiences, clients may relate to themselves and see how they may deal with their experiences on different occasions.

On balance, films may present different perspectives on an experience. Learning the observer's role may facilitate the process of gaining a broader mode of attention where the insula and dorsolateral prefrontal cortex are activated. The prefrontal cortex, as the most advanced part of the brain, would manifest itself in the act of observation and attention.

For a therapy to be implemented, therapists need to apply techniques to help clients follow through with practice discussions. In their broadest descriptive and illustrative scope, films may entail a wide variety of opportunities that espouse therapeutic dimensions. Films, for instance, may introduce models that help a client see the role of self-efficacy, assertiveness, bravery, benevolence, empowerment, and free will. Clients may be encouraged to watch a movie and embark on discovering, detecting, and examining suggested themes. Films can be generally taken as a text in its

4 Films as Learning Modules

broadest sense and can be examined as to both explicit and implicit meanings within the text.

Films may be discussed in terms of form and content, theme and plot, diction, and nonverbal components, including lighting, proxemics, setting, music, décor, mise-en-scène, staging, and costume. The focus can be explicitly or implicitly on a topic of importance. The movie may highlight the effect of a variable, the demonstration of a phenomenon, the process of a happening, and the role of internal and external factors.

Presenting the ingredients of an attitude in the context of emotional, behavioral, and cognitive factors may occur through a face-to-face meeting with a client followed by watching a movie such as the one suggested above.

The client can be encouraged to look for conversations, sentences, statements, interactions, scenes, moments, and episodes in the film that vivify an attitude's effect or representation. This might be a sentence, a paragraph, a gesture, a nonverbal cue, or the assemblage of all of these.

Movies may provide opportunities to explore the interplay of micro and macro elements in the social and political domains. Clients can be invited to look at a movie and see it as text that may entail a collection of meanings. In the examples mentioned above, therapists may call for a comparison of dialogues to demonstrate how meanings such as inferiority and superiority are linked to a sense of a self. The movies may decipher examples of self-construction and self-constriction through the tyranny of social contexts.

In general, a movie may be actively viewed for specific goals:

1 Films may cover certain problems such as physical or sexual abuse. *Bedeviled* (2016) and *Eden* (2016) are examples that move in line with this regard.
2 Films may concentrate on the nature of relationships and intimacy. Movies such as *The Notebook* (2004), *Blue Valentine* (2010), and *Before Midnight* (2013) fall into this category.
3 Films may bear upon physical and mental challenges. Movies such as *Silver Linings* (2012), *Playbook* (2012), *Girl, Interrupted* (1999), *Black Swan* (2010), *Rain Man* (1988), *A Beautiful Mind* (2001), *The Breakfast Club* (1985), *Good Will Hunting* (1997), and *Still Alice* (2014) are subsumed under this category.
4 Films may deal with values and ethics. *Mr. Smith Goes to Washington* (1939), *Gandhi* (1982), *An Ideal Husband* (1947), and *A Man for All Seasons* (1966) are representational in this connection.
5 Films may have depicted the phenomena of divorce and its implications. *Kramer vs. Kramer* (1979), *It Is Complicated* (2009), *Under the Tuscan Sun* (2003), *Mrs. Doubtfire* (1993), and *The Parent Trap* (1998) may be classified in this regard.
6 Films may provide examples and presentations of various forms of communication and conflict resolution. *Lincoln* (2012), *Thirteen Days*

Films as Learning Modules 5

(2000), *The Founder* (2016), and *Big Miracle* (2012) may be discussed under this category.

7   Films may portray and display posttraumatic stress disorder and its effects. *The Deer Hunter* (1978), *Coming Home* (1978), *Born on the Fourth of July* (1989), *Iron Man* (2008), *Saving Private Ryan* (1998), and *Mystic River* (2003) may be listed in this category.

8   Films may focus on the topic of religion and its manifestation. *Miracles Ffrom Heaven* (2016), *Martin Luther* (1953), *and Muhammad: The Messenger of God* (1976) may be cited in this category.

9   Films may purport the demonstration of tolerance of differences. *My Family* (1995), *Life of Pi* (2012), *Lost in Translation* (2003), and *Far and Away* (1992) are examples that move in line with this category.

10   Films may delineate eating disorders and their formation. *To the Bone* (2017), *Sharing the Secret* (2000), *Perfect Body* (1997), *For the Love of Nancy* (1994), and *A Secret Between Friends* (1996) may be included in this taxonomy.

11   Films may focus on anxiety and depression. *Little Miss Sunshine* (2006), *High Anxiety* (1977), *It's a Wonderful Life* (1946), and *The Hours* (2002) may be placed in this classification.

12   Films may picture the poignant tragedy of loss and grief. *Extremely Loud and Incredibly Close* (2011), *P.S. I Love You* (2007), and *Truly Madly Deeply* (1990) are on this list.

13   Films may point to having affairs in one's life. *Unfaithful* (2002), *Notes on a Scandal* (2006), *Little Children* (2006), *The Pian* (1993), and *The Seven Year Itch* (1955) present examples in line with this list.

14   Films may elucidate the issue of power and control and their effects. *Macbeth* (2015), *Wall Street* (1987), *The Last Emperor* (1987), and *The Last King of Scotland* (2006) may be included in this category.

15   Films may be used to discuss mental disorders, substance disorders, and diagnoses. For example, *Wall Street* (1987) for narcissistic personality disorder, *Young Adult* (2011) for borderline personality disorder, *Brassed Off* (1996) for adjustment disorder with depressed mood, *In Country* (1989) for posttraumatic stress disorder, *Dying to Dance* (2001) for anorexia nervosa, *Freeway II: Confessions of a Trickbaby* (1999) for bulimia nervosa, *Annie Hall* (1977) for generalized anxiety disorder, *Analyze This* (1999) for panic disorder, *The Hospital* (2013) for persistent depressive disorder, *Girl, Interrupted* (1999) for major depressive disorder, *Mad Love* (1995) for cyclothymic disorder, *Mr. Jones* (2019) and *Silver Linings Playbook* (2012) for bipolar I disorder, *A Beautiful Mind* (2001) for schizophrenia, *Flight* (2012) for alcohol and stimulant use disorder, *Blow* (2001) for stimulant use disorder, stimulant intoxication, stimulant withdrawal, affliction for alcohol use disorder, alcohol intoxication, and alcohol withdrawal.

6 Films as Learning Modules

A Beautiful Mind (2001).

In addition to the examples of films that are rife with sundry items and categories, there may be other examples that may illustrate how films can serve as a great forum for learning concepts, ideas, techniques, and skills.

The Hurricane (1999) offers a proactive approach against discrimination, injustice, and oppression. The film exhibits how saying "No" to oppressive powers may become possible through willpower, perseverance, and resistance.

The Shawshank Redemption (1994), *Papillon* (1973), and *Escape From Alcatraz* (1979) present how hope can serve as a panacea for overcoming problems.

The Perks of Being a Wallflower (2012) depicts the example of a movie with an elucidation of the role of anxiety and depression.

In *My Fair Lady* (1964), the process of change in one's behavior is portrayed with the indication of various factors that may transpire in the process of changing behavior.

In *Forest Gump* (1994), Forest Gump indicates his attitude by saying: "My Mama always said, 'Life was like a box of chocolates. You never know what you're gonna get.'"

In the movie *Lean on Me* (1989), social issues and education are discussed in line with one another. The clients can be invited to reflect on the relationship between macro and microelements of change and education. The following quotes from the movie may demonstrate a few examples of opportunities to expand reflective and reflexive thinking:

JOE CLARK: They used to call me Crazy Joe. Well, now they can call me Batman!

JOE CLARK: You are not inferior. Your grades may be. Your school may have been. However, you can turn all that around and make liars out of those bastards in exactly one hour when you take that test, pass it, and win!

Films as Learning Modules 7

The above-cited example in *Lean on Me* (1989) may be discussed and examined in connection with a distinction between what is in mind and being the owner of the mind: one may be owned by one's mind, and one may become the owner of the mind. When the mind owns you, you may see your full dependency on the mind, whereas when you learn to be the owner of the mind, you may see your role in accepting or challenging what the mind is prescribing.

In *Guess Who's Coming to Dinner* (1967), the movie displays an attitude and its implications. An *attitude*, psychologically speaking, is about an evaluation: an evaluation of someone, something, an event, or a phenomenon.

It may be time to reiterate at this stage that the substance of the learning modules as discussed here lies in observational learning. Observational learning associated with Albert Bandura's name as the pioneer of the field explicates the vital role of observation in the process of learning.

One does not need to do something to learn it; one can observe an action to learn it. This demonstrates the powerful function of films in producing templates, scripts, schemas, and lifestyles. Films can therefore espouse an unrivaled medium for learning in diversified domains. The domains can include behaviors, attitudes, values, feelings, thoughts and cognitions, living modes, etc.

On another level, films can define how the world is, how the world should be, and how the world could have been. Films can present and represent different worlds with different compartments.

Films can also display the gaps between the real world, the ideal world, and the world built upon others' oughts. Likewise, films can decipher and unearth the antinomies of different worlds. Antagonistic clashes of different worlds can be illustrated in films. These worlds can entail the subjective experiences of people and their phenomenologically lived world.

Discovering the cynosure of the worlds that films have constructed may also reveal the impact of constructivism and constructionism: two viewers may see two different things from a scene and interpret them differently. In the meantime, the viewers' interpretations take place in accordance with their contextually constructed worlds, namely, their social, cultural, economic, political, and personal worlds.

Therapists may encourage clients to reflect on the constructed worlds of films and ask them to see how the constructed world can be deconstructed through the client's deconstructionism. The power of deconstructing the film's construction will allow the client to increase his or her metacognition competencies, critical thinking, and mindfulness.

In following the learning and educational facet of films, therapists can introduce certain movies based on the goal, the direction and nature of therapy, the client's status quo, and the essence of their problems and issues. In doing so, therapists may focus on the entire film or specific scenes to discuss the following questions (please note that each question needs to be discussed in its context and view of the client's situational analysis):

8   Films as Learning Modules

1 What is it that you see as the general message of the film?
2 How do you see the relationship between each character's feelings and his or her action in a particular scene?
3 How do you see the relationship between each character's thinking and his or her action?
4 What would you have done under similar circumstances?
5 What else could the character have done under the circumstances?
6 What can you elicit from what you view in such scenes?
7 If you took the film script and change any parts of that, what would you change?
8 How do you see the relationship between the film and real-life situations?
9 Are there any things in the film that you may think can be discussed as a common element among people in general?
10 How do you see the impact of one's perspective in relation to what is happening?
11 Do you see any connection between what is happening in the scene with more significant and macro levels beyond the particular scene?
12 Based on the particular scene of our discussion, do you see a mindless or a mindful behavior (discussions on mindfulness and mindlessness are presented later in this book)?
13 Based on our discussion's particular scene, how do you see the role of language in influencing the interaction?
14 Based on our discussion's particular scene, how do you see the choice of words in creating positive or negative emotions?
15 Based on our discussion's particular scene, can you see the elements of nonverbal behavior in influencing the interactions?
16 Based on the particular scene of our discussion, how do you see the role of awareness toward nonverbal behavior as helpful in influencing an interaction?
17 Based on our discussion's particular scene, do you observe any inconsistency in what is said and what is displayed in the behavior?
18 Based on the particular scene of our discussion (if it is a movie that can entail virtues and personal strengths with a positive psychological theme), do you think that the character(s) can help you adopt a better coping strategy in dealing with your problem?
19 Based on our discussion's particular scene, do you see any inspirational message that can enlighten you?
20 If you can think of yourself as the director of your own life as a film, how would you implement your direction? Do you decompose or recompose your own life as a text?
21 When watching the film, did you notice the flux of your own emotions? Did you experience positive or negative emotions?
22 Do you agree that emotions are contagious? How do you see the role of the film in producing, developing, or spreading specific emotions?

Films as Learning Modules 9

23 Based on the particular scene of our discussion, do you see the presence of emotional management?

24 Based on our discussion's particular scene, do you think that others would have done what the character(s) did?

25 Based on our discussion's particular scene, do you think the character's emotions ran the character, or did he or she manage their emotions?

26 Based on our discussion's particular scene, do you see the character acting authentically, or do you see his or her action merely as pretentiousness?

27 Based on our discussion's particular scene, do you see any application of the character's performance in a real-life situation?

28 Based on our discussion's particular scene, do you see any coping strategy that may be helpful in real-life situations?

29 Based on our discussion's particular scene, do you see any intrapersonal issue, or do you see any interpersonal problem?

30 Based on the particular scene of our discussion, how do you feel about the overall interaction?

2 Films and Psychoanalysis

Films may be examined and discussed in numerous therapeutic contexts. One of the primary contexts of film analysis may be allocated to psychoanalysis.

Psychoanalysis and film have a common history: *Studies in Hysteria* was published in 1895 (see Freud & Brill, 2015) with the emergence of psychoanalysis in Vienna, which was simultaneous with the world's first motion picture screening by the Lumiere Brothers in Paris. Correspondingly, both psychoanalysis and films have revolutionized our understanding of ourselves and our psychic dynamics and have opened up new horizons of exploration in understanding the human mind, human unconsciousness, and human psyche.

Mulvey (1976) brought psychoanalysis into film theory in the 1970s. Lacan's (1994) impact was more noticeable through film theory's use of Lacanian psychoanalytical terms in the 1970s. Topics such as the analysis of spectatorship, filmmakers' unconscious dynamics, and cultural mythology have been discussed and analyzed in light of the psychoanalytical theories and films.

Earlier than that, Harvard psychologist Hugo Münsterberg (1970) argued in his book *Film: A Psychological Study* that there can be a direct relationship between films and the psychological mechanisms, including imagination, emotion, attention, and memory. Films served as a great tool to present the relationship between reality and fantasy, the conscious and the unconscious mind.

According to psychoanalytic theory, personality structure is composed of three parts: the id, the ego, and the super ego. The id operates based on the pleasure principle and understands no language except the language of enjoyment and pleasure. When a hungry child cries, the only way to soothe him or her is to offer to breastfeed. You can't read poetry to the child to calm him or her. With the development of personality, the ego germinates. The language of the ego is based on the reality principle. In other words, the pleasure principle can no longer be operable. Norms, laws, regulations, rules, etc., do not allow the person to gallop the horses of the id unbridled. When a desire transpires, the ego takes into account

DOI: 10.4324/9780429441431-2

the reality principle and does not allow the id to proceed freely. Thus, one does not start itching oneself in front of people whenever the urge arrives. One considers the inappropriateness of the action because of the presence of the others. The super ego constitutes the other dimension of personality, which acts based on the punishment and reward system. If one abides by the rules set out by the ego and societal rules, rewards appear with the production of good feelings, whereas the violation of the instructions would produce guilt and shame.

Psychoanalysis centers on anxiety and its overarching destructive power. The constant flux of anxiety espouses pathology and defense mechanisms such as projection, repression, denial, rationalization, intellectualization, repression, reaction formation, sublimation (as the only healthy mechanisms), and so forth that occur unconsciously to help the person cope with anxiety. Anxiety is thus the forcible and formidable element that takes control of people in various forms and contextualization.

Psychoanalysis also propounds that most people's behaviors are done unconsciously. People may be aware of one layer of their behavior in the conscious facet but unaware of the unconscious components. The unconscious may demonstrate itself and display itself through different means, including an association of ideas, slips of the tongue, jokes and humor, dreams and movies, cinema and films.

Clients may be encouraged to watch films with a psychoanalytical theme to grasp the concepts, techniques, and dynamics of the psyche.

In *I Confess* (1953), layers of the unconscious, the conflicts between different parts of the personality, anxiety, and defense mechanisms, are richly available.

The client can be invited to watch a particular film and see how the relationship between the unconscious parts of the behavior and its implications in one's life may be meticulously tracked. In doing so, the goal is not to attribute the theme or the happening or a character's traits to the clients but to develop an awareness that there may be roots unknown to us in terms of our behavior.

A behavior is meant to broadly encompass all forms of actions, thoughts, feelings, and emotions that may occur in an interpersonal or intrapersonal context. In *Marnie* (1964), for example, the girl charter starts yelling and crying in horror upon observing specific scenes and colors unbeknownst to her and her newly met husband. After the analysis of the roots, it is only after the roots that it turns out to be a relationship between her display of petrification and intimidation and her childhood observation of what happened to her mom on a stormy night. Films, in this connection, may unveil cryptic and clandestine parts of realities that may have been concealed to oblivion, negligence, or ignorance.

Apart from the idiosyncratic features of a film that may comply with the explanatory topics of psychoanalysis or their exegesis in terms of the application or implications of psychoanalytical tools, the mere attention

12   *Films and Psychoanalysis*

toward detecting and procuring the complex psychological interactions in a film may tend to increase the level of awareness for a client and may help him or her to enhance his or her level of metacognition, understanding, analysis, synthesis, and perspective making.

The following suggestions may be used to prompt the direction of the enhanced awareness for clients.

Clients may be invited to watch a film (naming a film appropriate to the psychoanalytical theory) and list several layers of behavior that may be interconnected to another behavior's unconscious dimension that may be seemingly unrelated. For instance, in *Marnie* (1964), the girl's overreactive responses with sudden physiological changes may seem to be unrelated or insensible on the surface, but deep down they convey multifarious realms of sensibility.

Clients can watch a given film and see how one may be unconsciously unaware of one's doings. Movies such as *Black Swan* (2010) present and demonstrate the unconscious world's implications for one's behaviors.

Clients may be encouraged to dig into deeper layers of meanings besides the ordinary dimensions of meaning. This may help the client understand the distinction between the core meanings and the marginal, affective, and associative meanings. A core meaning refers to what the word's denotation is all about. However, the marginal meanings loom in their sensibility with reference to other surrounding realms, which may be partly or mostly coming from the unconscious. In *Citizen Kane* (1941), the word *Rosebud* is not confined to the denotative meaning as it opens us the avenues of scrutinizing the past and its impacts on one's life.

Clients may be invited to see the observer's role versus the actor through watching the interplay of the dynamics of the psyche in connection with varying forms of experiences. For instance, *Psycho* (1960) portrays numerous elements of involvement in the deeper realm of self. The singular self appears to be embedded within the interwoven process of the unconscious and the conscious. The movie can foster the spirit of thoughtfulness for questions on agency, choice, self-regulation, and self-management.

The psychoanalytical focus on films may concentrate on different attribution levels in the conscious and the unconscious parts. The conscious part in *Psycho* (1960) takes us to the signification of episodes in the manifest layers with the highlights of elements such as theft, escape, and guilt. On the unconscious part, the film leads us to the complex avenues of the signifiers and the signified in a potpourri of layers beyond the conventionally identified paradigms.

Psychoanalytical examination of films may delineate how the subjects in a plot may secure assignments other than the regular assignments necessary to constitute a narrative. In *Psycho* (1960), for instance, Norman serves as a subject in a hotel owner's context in one level. However, in a unique level of assignment, he is operating as someone whose internal skirmishes embitter his outlook toward the world.

The Birds (1963).

In *The Birds* (1963), the woman turns out to be a customer looking for some birds in the assignment's general stance. In another exclusive assignment, she symbolizes the one who imports a protesting voice and an insurgent messenger with objection and upsurge.

Psychoanalytical hermeneutics of films may generate an emblem toward different stages of awareness with the reiteration that reality is not what is seen in the obvious level. Movies such as *Shadow of a Doubt* (1943) can present an interplay of interconnected cryptically operative elements that dig into complex levels of the conscious and the unconscious phenomenology.

The opening piece from the movie *Secrets of a Soul* (1926) may voice the propensity toward psychoanalysis. The opening reads as follows: "Inside every person, there are desires and passions which remain unknown to 'consciousness.'"

According to Metz & Britton (1982), psychoanalytical examination of a film would presage the influence of the unconscious in our lives.

> At the cinema, it is always the other who is on the screen; as for me, I am there to look at him. I take no part in the perceived, on the contrary, I am all-perceiving. All perceiving as one says, all-powerful (this is the famous gift of "ubiquity" the film gives its spectator); all-perceiving, too, because I am entirely on the side of the perceiving instance: absent from the screen, but certainly present in the auditorium, a great eye and ear without which the perceived would have no one to perceive it, the instance, in other words, which constitutes the cinema signifier (it is I who make the film).
>
> (p. 48)

14 *Films and Psychoanalysis*

The spectator and the film's dialectics develop a significant place in the psychoanalytical study of the film. The role of the other and the Other, along with the Lacanian understanding of symbol, real, and the imaginary, would constitute the main axes of the analysis. The psychoanalytic theory after the 1970s considered cinema and film as an institution or an apparatus. This theory, known as *apparatus theory*, was distinctly different from previous approaches that demonstrated an interest in clandestine and hidden or repressed meanings in the film text.

Jean-Louis Baudry, Christian Metz, and Laura Mulve, who were part of the psychoanalytical movement after the 1970s, discussed the relationship between film and the audience, with cinema acting as the manifestation of an ideology. Right after Baudry and his allies, the feminist, psychoanalytical theory led by Laura Mulvey appeared with its challenge against Baudry's and Metz's work. Metz and Baudry discussed desire in the context of the male Oedipal trajectory, something that feminist psychoanalytical theory did not like: feminist theories examined the question of constructing the viewers in connection with gender and sexual desire.

After the feminist approach, another trend with a psychoanalytical orientation concentrated on critical studies of the female Oedipal trajectory, masculinity and masochism, fantasy theory and spectatorship, and woman as active, sadistic monster. Finally, psychoanalytic film theory raised its voice in combination with postcolonial theory and body theory and other critical approaches.

Each of these approaches brings its own scope of focus and attention and examines films in view of their postulated axioms. The apparatus theory, for instance, elaborated the role of cinema as an institution with its own agenda and influence, which also created a piece of mental machinery.

One of the main engagements of film's psychoanalytic theory unfolds itself in the relationship between spectator and cinema. The analysis can be embedded within Lacanian psychoanalysis, where there are different stages of development, namely, the imaginary, the symbolic, and the real. In the imaginary stage, the child looks at the mirror and observes his or her image. The image gives the child a sense of a fully formed self but only at the perfunctory level. The child recognizes himself and, in the meantime, is stuck in the misrecognition. He understands but misunderstands. This is the beginning of the split.

Likewise, the audience in the cinema identifies with the characters on the screen. The identification takes place with misunderstanding since the subject of identification being an idealized self in the form of a splendid star is not tantamount to the viewer's reality. The dialectics of recognition and misrecognition, understanding, and misunderstanding transpires here.

Lacanian psychoanalysis underlines the gap between understanding and misunderstanding and its implications. The mirror stage would espouse a concentrated gaze at the external, the outside, and the exterior parts of

Films and Psychoanalysis 15

life. For this reason, people may sum up their energy in taking care of the outside in order to impress others. Fashions and obsession with weight and body are the by-products of this outside-oriented component of the self. This, however, leads to the development of a pseudo and elusive self that is devoid of a genuine connectedness to its inner world.

Lacan's discussion of the imaginary, the symbolic, and the real in the human psyche may be further elaborated with attention toward the specificity of the imaginary as an order or a stage where fullness and completion are imagined. The imaginary order entails our wishes, fantasies, and images in our psyche functions from birth until somewhere around 6 months. The mother dominates the imaginary order. This is when people experience joy and unification with their mother as they receive everything from her, including nourishment, care, love, comfort, and tranquility. Images are the centerpiece of our perception and interpretation in this stage, which serves as a preverbal stage. The images are constantly and incessantly moving. The mirror stage arrives between 6 and 18 months, and Lacan calls this the mirror stage. Babies see themselves in a mirror. This image brings an illusion since babies are not really in control of themselves but might assume otherwise. The illusion is expanded throughout life. In this stage, we understand the object petit a, which implies the separation of some of the objects from us. The separation of these objects brings us the longing to have them, so we yearn for them since they are not present. This sense of lack continues to operate in the entire parts of our life. The symbolic order arrives with the presence of the father, who brings us the language. The symbolic order is occupied by the father. Language emerges in the symbolic order. The relationship between language and us is a relationship of mastery and subjugation: language controls us, constructs our identity, and shapes us. The real order comes next. The real order encompasses everything in the physical and the material world, but in the meantime, it entails innumerable object petit a, namely, objects that testify to the symbolic conceptualization of lacking.

Lacan's emphasis on the lack and its implications for human beings in their entire life may also purport that films and cinema with their provocative and evocative roles in bringing to mind the order of the imaginary may bring a delectable sense of consummation as it reverberates the remembrance and reminiscence of the imaginary. In other words, films may carry their power to bring jouissance, giving rise to a recollection of a time when wholeness and unification were paramount. The joy of that observation in the human psyche may be conspicuously triggered by films.

In discussing the psychoanalytical facets of films, therapists may encourage clients to ponder and reflect on the following questions:

1   Are there levels of interactions in the film that may suggest a connection to the unconscious part? Alfred Hitchcock's *Psycho* (1960) and *Marnie* (1964) present powerful examples where the psychoanalytical

16 *Films and Psychoanalysis*

layers of the unconscious for the boy and the girl unfold rigorous themes for discussion.

2 Are there examples in the film where complex relationships of the unconscious are portrayed? *The Student of Prague* (1913) is an old example that can be discussed here. *Dr. Mobuse* (1933) and *Split* (2016) are other examples that may unearth the clandestine world of the unconscious.

3 How does the relationship between the conscious and the unconscious transpire in the interactions of the film? *The Clockwork Orange* (1971), *Shame* (2011), and *Repulsion* (1965) can be discussed in this connection.

4 What are the signs of an allusion to the unconscious spheres in the film?

5 Are there examples of defense mechanisms in the films that reveal themselves? The *Science of Sleep* (2006) and *Black Swan* (2010) can be mentioned as two examples.

6 How do the Lacanian symbol order and the role of language highlight our embeddedness within language?

7 In discussing the conflicts in the interpersonal or intrapersonal realms, what specific aspects of relationships have been ignored, neglected, abused, or undermined?

3 Films and Mindfulness

People may watch a film mindlessly; that is, in an automatic manner, without paying any attention to the present moment. In other words, people may passively view a film and perceive the content without any active role in interpreting and analyzing the content. Here, they simply move based on their previously established priming, remembering, and judging in accordance with their programmed taxonomy of perception and recollection. The opposite may happen when viewers watch a film mindfully with an intentional focus on the present moment. They do not let themselves be at the mercy of what the film wants them to see. Their attention is proactive but not constricted.

In different forms of mindfulness, including meditation-based mindfulness and Langerian critical mindfulness, the goal is to develop an intentional, flexible, open, and presence-oriented attention that can act proactively.

Meditation-based mindfulness, which is mainly characterized through the works of John Kabat-Zinn (2003a, 2003b, 2005) and is also associated with mindfulness-based stress reduction (MBSR), highlight the role of meditation in achieving mindfulness.

Langerian mindfulness, rooted in tens of empirically validated experiments, argues that mindfulness can also be obtainable through non-meditation-based components (see Langer, 1989, 2005, 2009).

Perspective is of great significance in understanding Langerian mindfulness. It may be the underlying element of one's indulgence in a repetitive course of living interwoven with helplessness, anxiety, fear, isolation, and negativity. However, a change of perspective can create a new course of action where responsibility, responsiveness, proactivity, choice, and empowerment can give rise to a novel mode of being.

From a therapeutic point of view, clients can be encouraged to see how multiple perspectives may make sense in a film.

For instance, in *Kramer vs. Kramer* (1979), you may see two different perspectives with different claims and different implications. Mindfulness would allow people to go beyond one single perspective. This often helps clients to see the power of empathy in reaching someone else's outlook.

DOI: 10.4324/9780429441431-3

18 Films and Mindfulness

Guess Who's Coming to Dinner (1967).

In *Grapes of Wrath* (1940), you may also see how an event may bring people together in sharing a perspective that may not have been easily noticed prior to the event.

Such films may help clients to see how broadening the perspective may be of great avail in displaying the power of empathy. It may also help them to see how a shift of perspective may give rise to growth-oriented consequences.

In *A Patch of Blue* (1965) and *Guess Who's Coming to Dinner* (1967), the films present great resources for thoughtfulness, mindfulness, and a shift of perspectives. Clients may be encouraged to watch the films and discuss the impact of looking from a different perspective or celebrating multiple perspectives.

The proactive nature of mindfulness may begin with re-examining the mindset. Many empirically based experiments indicate that people lose their creativity and agency when placed in a state of mindlessness and merely succumb to a passive mode of reactivity (see Langer, 1989, 2002, 2005, 2009). Mindfulness enhancement would help people notice their power of creativity, their choices in making a decision, their efficacy in dealing with challenges, and their novelty in improving their performance (see Fatemi et al., 2016).

In other words, mindlessness would deprive people of questioning the dominant discourses of their lives, whether these discourses have been brought to them through their upbringing, schooling, culture, environment, or even therapeutic discourses.

So, people can mindlessly follow the patterns of stories created for them by others without realizing their own power to change the story. Mindfulness begins with an active state of mind. Our passive, reactive, and automatic state

Films and Mindfulness 19

of mind changes into an active and proactive state in experiencing mindfulness.

This state is characterized through noticing new things, exploring novelty, and looking at the unfamiliar. It is creational. We create while we are mindful. In addition, mindfulness fosters an awareness of the context. As mindfulness expands, we become more sensitive to context. The past does not overdetermine the present.

We pay attention to the rules, but we are not governed by them. The rules can be guiding but are not paralyzing. Mindfulness activates the experiential and phenomenological connectedness to the present moment. When mindful, we live in the moment: we experience a full engagement at the moment. Our presence is consummated through mindfulness (Langer, 2005, 2009).

Mindfulness influences one's way of being, one's existential and ontological mode (Langer, 2000, 2005). Mindfulness provides the possibility of bridging the gap between the inner and outer worlds, where one ascertains the possibility of influencing both realms.

Langerian mindfulness as an approach proposes that control goes away when one is mindlessly disconnected from him- or herself. When mindless, one is constricted in an inflexible state of mind where one is steeped in an emotional, cognitive, and behavioral paralysis.

This paralysis limits the power of control and imposes helplessness and desperation as the only functional parameters of being.

Mindfulness entails an experiential acknowledgment of one's empowerment in the creative process of reshaping one's cognitive, emotional, and behavioral options. It is tied to the phenomenological engagement of understanding possibilities beyond the pre-established patterns of identification.

Langerian mindfulness argues that as soon as one is able to notice novelty in one's status quo, one will be able to discern the possibility of disengagement from the status quo. For instance, if a person is solely defined in his professional role as a chairperson and is so fully immersed in his being nothing but a chair, this definition will impose an entrenchment of being nothing except a chair. If the chairship is taken away for any reason, the person perceives himself as doomed to failure since his self-definition source has been degraded.

Films can demonstrate how obedience to rampant forms of stories may deprive people of going beyond their status quo. *Zapata* (1970) and *Robinhood* (2018) are two examples that describe how social and political movements can be borne in the hearts of questioning the dominant political discourses.

The problem with dominantly established mindlessness is that it does not allow people to see anything except the direction given to them. Once you get yourself locked into some information, you may not be able to see anything else except the given information.

20 *Films and Mindfulness*

Movies can provide a rich repertoire of examples with a meticulous tilt toward mindfulness and mindlessness in interpersonal, intrapersonal, and macro levels of life.

Viewers can be subjugated to dominant therapeutic discourses, too. When mindless, the viewers would move in line with that dominant discourse. Viewers can mindfully watch a film and instead of abiding by the repeatedly pervasive categories, they can proactively observe, describe, and express their chosen way of analysis. When mindless, for instance, viewers may watch a violent film and merely go by the violent effects, thus performing violently in action.

Mindfulness challenges the domineering discourses and questions their universality. Langerian doctrine of mindfulness requires understanding the specific contexts of the action, behaviors, feelings, and episodes in a film.

The contextual understanding of perspectives and plots in a film would require an in-depth exploration of their uniqueness. Examining the context would also take place through the rigorous and mindful understanding of the film's language: what is it that films tell people, what is maximized or minimized in their stories, how does the film's language contribute to the empowerment or disempowerment of people, how is the film's language influenced by a macro language coming from their culture, upbringing, education, political, and economic system? What is the language that the films have been using, or what language have they been subscribed to use?

Labels bring mindlessness (see Langer, 2009). Clients can be mindlessly subjected to a passive mode of living through complying with labels attributed to them in either the macro or micro level. From a Langerian perspective, dominant therapeutic discourses can also impose mindlessness through creating a reference point where the client's context is marginalized and his or her voice is lost.

> When we learn mindlessly, we look at experience and impose a contingent relationship between two things—what we or someone else did and what we think happened as a result. We interpret that experience from a single perspective, oblivious to the other ways it can be seen. Mindful learning looks at experience and understands that it can be seen in countless ways. New information is always available, and that more than one perspective is both possible and extremely valuable. It's an approach that leads us to be careful about what we "know" to be true and how we learn it. At the level of the particular experience, each event is unique.
>
> (pp. 29–30)

Langer (1975, 2005, 2009, 1989, 1997) indicated that mindfulness helps us become more sensitive to context and it brings us mastery of our actions to the effect that we experience our agency in our decision-making process.

Langer (2000) considered mindfulness as something that liberates us from our limitations and allows us to learn as creatively and openly as possible. On the other hand, she indicated that mindlessness is not only an impediment for novel ideas and distinctions but is also imposing mindsets "that have been mindlessly accepted to be true".

Our habituated ways of knowing may strongly keep us in a process where the emotional, cognitive, and behavioral mechanisms from the past over-determine the present moment and therefore our experience of the moment is victimized through the flux of the past combinatory elements. This may have different implications for limiting, distorting, containing, incarcerating, and constricting our present experience to the effect that the experiential process may be detached from the nature of the present experience. Instead of experiencing the taste of an apple in the immediate now and the moment, for instance, the taste might remind us of a previously experienced flavor or it might give the recollection of our grandparents' garden of apples. In any case, we become devoid of the present moment.

Langerian mindfulness argues for a state of mind that can get fully connected to the moment while remaining flexibly open to exploring the moment's flow and its multiple possibilities. This is the vital ingredient of Langerian mindfulness, which generates a genuine sense of presence. Presence entails a mental, cognitive, emotional, behavioral, and overall existential preparation to examine and get engaged in the immediate now. In this sense, Langerian mindfulness is not merely about cognition but is an ontological shift where one may experience the radical transformation of consciousness.

This involves a shift of attention in a choice oriented mode that can facilitate management of attention. The choice is the key ingredient of mindfulness: with an enhancement of mindfulness, one learns to see the implementation of choice and the power of selective attentiveness. In an absent-oriented mode or mindlessness, attention is scattered and sporadic.

Langerian mindfulness offers a special tilt in the experiential and phenomenological process of connectedness to the present moment. The presence is of great significance here as it provides the essence of "being there." The athlete who is there experiences the unifying theme of presence away from multiplicity, absence, and sporadic cognitive and emotional engagements.

Langer's revolutionary concept of mindfulness demonstrates that presence is mostly concealed to oblivion through mindless multitasking, incarceration within one perspective, inflexibility in revising one's position of being, and lack of authenticity at the moment-to-moment experiential presentation of self.

When mindlessness is rampant, one lives and acts in absentia: one is all over the place; one fails to experience the panacea of lively connectedness to the present moment as the occupation with the past or the future would prevent one from an active lingering at the moment.

Mindfulness blooms in presence and through presence. It unifies the aptitudes, abilities, competencies, and skills into one and allows one to

22 *Films and Mindfulness*

experience the wholeness of him- or herself in the interconnectedness of action and the agent. The subjective experience and the objective experience intermingle with one another, and the dichotomy of the subject–object relationship ceases to operate. The wholeness within the experiential process of mindfulness is intertwined with the consequential ontological transformation of consciousness where being and mindfulness consummate together.

In the absence, multiplicities grow in that the focus is gone and the perspective management ceases to operate. With the rise of multiplicities, one may experience fragmentation where the fullness of attention goes away and presence is replaced by absence. Absence is degenerating wholeness and brings about division. You may be physically there but not psychologically there, or you may be cognitively there but not emotionally there.

The goal of mindfulness is to create and promote a whole-oriented presence where the full-fledged presence may open up viewing multiple possibilities. When in mindfulness, one may enjoy the benefit of connectedness to the immediate now. The preconceived mindset of possibility may keep the sensibility of possibility within the predetermined mapping of possibility and thus limits the meaningfulness of possibility based on the paradigmatic analysis of the previously established categories. If you had gone to people a hundred years ago and discussed with them the possibility of making an iPhone in the present format, people would have described it, perhaps with derision, as impossible.

This may transpire in a group of athletes through a promotional prompt of communication where everyone is asked to disengage from the scattered shower of multiplicities and massiveness of mental preoccupations. The tale of the Oxford rowing crew's 1987 race against Cambridge may elucidate the vitality of such moments (Topolski, 1989, cited in Schneider et al., 2012).

After losing the race in 1986, the Oxford boat club faced a long year before meeting Cambridge again. Aside from the wounded pride and standard training, those 12 months included an inordinate amount of drama. One of the 1986 Oxford crew members, an American named Chris Clarke, returned the following year with several experienced American rowers who had enrolled in Oxford. Simply, their plan was to put out as strong a team as they could, one that could not possibly lose to Cambridge again.

As often happens in sports, things did not go as planned. The team had little camaraderie, and members even showed outright hostility toward each other and the club's leaders. The newer rowers did not agree with the established training routines; they felt that the training routines were not necessary to ensure success. Disagreements over training methods resulted in an attempt to oust the club president (who also rowed on the team). When this revolt failed, half of the team members, led by the American contingent, quit the club with just 6 weeks to go before the boat race.

A poorly trained, substandard crew was left to prepare for the race. The team showed no unity, had little confidence in leaders, and was largely disinterested in the race. Training runs and exhibition competitions resulted in poor times, further decreasing team confidence. Team members admitted to each other that they had little chance of winning the race and provided a wide variety of reasons for this impending failure.

However, the team did not fail. Instead, it pulled off a historic upset victory against Cambridge. From a social psychological perspective, one key aspect of this triumph was that, during a final team retreat, the team voted on the line-up for the race with Cambridge, inserting the maligned club president into a key potion in the boat. Although time was running out from that point onward, the crew's training performances were excellent (Topolski, 1989, cited in Schneider et al., 2012).

This may be further studied in view of the prompt mode of communication, where one may see the coach's attempt to disengage the crew from mindless entrapment. Addressing the team, the coach said: "'This is your weather,' I told the crew," and

> out there it's your water- no one can cope with those waves like you guys can, at least of all Cambridge. You have the weight and technique for rough water-and better still, and you have the nerve for it. And, I don't think Cambridge has that nerve. If it stays like this, I really think you could pull it off tomorrow.
> (Topolski, 1989, cited in Schneider et al., 2012, pp. 274–275)

The story mentioned above may explicate the importance of influencing one's performance through developing a sense of connectedness to the significance of the present moment and its potential resources. This may be facilitated through a motivational speech, as was done in this case. On an individual level, too, one may leap beyond the mindlessly accepted self-talk of negativity and helplessness and engage in productive, proactive, and positive self-talk.

Langerian mindfulness propounds that thoughts can be taken as a series of choices and choices are ultimately changeable. The sovereignty of the recursive parade of mindlessly accepted thoughts would impose an unquestionable and indubitable obedience to them. One can't stop paying attention to them, and right after the attention, the endorsement happens.

According to Langerian mindfulness, paying attention to thought is a choice. One can always choose not to choose this choice. Furthermore, one may choose to attend to the thought but choose not to endorse the thought. With an increase of mindfulness and its components, including noticing new things and increasing the experiential and phenomenological presence at the moment, one would be able to ascertain and acknowledge the power of agency, namely, the power of one's choices over the context.

Mindlessness suggests the availability of no power and no agency. It is equipped with the automatic regurgitation of loss of power and devoid of

24 Films and Mindfulness

agency. Mindless-driven performance is entrenched within the habitual powerlessness of the past's tyranny, so in Langerian doctrine, the past overdetermines the present, and there is no presence except the precipitating effects of the past stricken presence.

Back to the tale of the Oxford rowing crew's 1987 race against Cambridge: The coach wages his endeavor to bring the focus of the team to the present moment. He then inspires them with the power of choices and hopefulness. Langer's experiments (1975, 1989, 1997, 2005, 2009; Langer & Abelson, 1974; Langer et al., 1978, 1985) have indicated that with an increase in mindfulness, one would be able to have more influence to empower others. It is interesting to know that mindfulness opens up the way for activating moments of connectedness to both the inner world and the external world. On the other hand, social psychologists and researchers who have studied performance indicate that positive messages and enhancement of conversations among team members between and during plays, expression of emotions, and team cohesion are positively correlated with positive performance (see Dale & Wrisberg, 1996; DiBerardinis et al., 1983; Lausic et al., 2009; Sullivan & Feltz, 2003; Widmeyer & Williams, 1991).

Langerian mindfulness highlights the psychological ontology of being there as an essential element of a peak performance. The corollary of the psychological ontology purports a perceptive and sagacious distancing from the familiar avenues of being with a search for the unfamiliar.

Thus, mindfulness ends up being about the being itself and not cognition or emotion. When performance and being are mutually tied to the fountains of wholeness in the moment, the performance will intrinsically move in the heart of expansive mindfulness. In other words, mindfulness expands ontologically and experientially. With the expansion of each moment where the performer experiences the fullness of the link to the presence, his or her performance increases. It is like walking over a mountain where each step allows you to be more in touch with new horizons of possibilities.

According to Langerian mindfulness, these horizons are sequentially and simultaneously giving rise to different stages of mindfulness to the effect that each stage is enriching the scope and breadth of the previous stage, and hence liminal spaces are discovered through the expansion of the creative moments. Liminal spaces are unknown to the mindlessly calculated parameters; they are unbeknownst to the logically driven mentality. Yet, they unfold themselves as the process of present-oriented vivacity increases. In doing so, outcome goals, process goals, and performance goals are united in the interactive process of mindfulness and living in the moment.

Films may impose mindlessness through prescribing politically definitive modes of living. This might happen in conscious and or subliminal levels.

In *High School Musical* (2008), *Friends* (2011), and *Batman Begins* (2005), you may see how a specific discourse is highlighted as the pervasive discourse with characteristic features of power, attraction, and excellence.

Films and Mindfulness 25

Language plays a pivotal role in creating mindfulness (see Fatemi, 2018). Language is not just an instrument or a device to make transactions: it entails a mode of being. When mindless, people are incarcerated within a language that seems to be unchangeable and unavoidable. For people with depression, this language produces sadness, fear, anxiety, and helplessness (Davidson, 2000). This language unfolds itself in the paramount emotions of people with depression. The use of a counterproductive language epitomized in the barrage of negative emotions would impede the process of deconstructing the language from the user of the language: the person strongly identifies him- or herself with the language, and he or she cannot disengage him- or herself from the emotions generated by the underlying negative emotions.

Paying attention to the language used in a film may help the client see how the language choice or subscription to a language chosen may produce differing consequences. This language may unfold its manifestation in the obvious forms of interactions and conversations or the deeply innate layers of societal and cultural modes of being and living.

Night on Earth (1991) and *Party* (1968) may be examined in terms of their language use in pointing to different forms of realities in different perspectives. They may also decipher how structural components of the social and political pillars may contribute to the production of different modes of expressiveness.

Langerin mindfulness starts with helping the client notice perspectives that may not be available in the person's repertoire with, say, depression. The client is encouraged to explore the possibilities of alternative modes of perspectives. When depressed or stressed, people experience negative interpretation bias: they see more negative aspects than positive sides. This may lead to their actions from a single perspective that does not allow them to see any other modes of possibilities except what they are enmeshed in.

The Langerian mindfulness commencement point lies in delineating the relationship between one's perspective and one's mode of existence. Mindlessly lived stories do not leave any room for attention to variability. Helping clients understand how perspectives can be limited and limiting would allow them to see the implications of their phenomenologically lived stories.

Sunset Boulevard (1950) may be cited as a strenuous example of how not questioning the embedded mindlessness in one's story may keep one from looking at alternative modes of perspectives. Films entail *a what* and *a how*. In discussing the what of films, clients examine the events, their sequential order, and their syntagmatic analysis and focus on what it is that has occurred, namely, the content of the films.

In focusing on how films are displayed, clients are encouraged to fathom the discourse of the films. How the films are presented, their modes of display, and their modes of presentation are pronounced here.

26   *Films and Mindfulness*

The presentation here includes both the verbal, vocal, and visual parts of the films. How the film is presented, represented, and displayed and the representational features in the film constitute the film's discourse.

In understanding the films' implications for real-life situations, clients can learn to see their own stories' discourses (how they are told) and their implications.

A story's discourse can be limiting, oppressive, and paralyzing. Langerian mindfulness would help clients realize how the content and the discourse of their stories can mindlessly impede the process of looking into the unnoticed features of their stories. When fraught with depression, anxiety, fear, and doubts, clients may neglect the realm of alternative possibilities that may be available to them. Mindlessness would circumscribe the horizon of possibilities by narrowing down the agency behind people's stories.

Langerian mindfulness would help clients understand the process of separating themselves from the dominant discourse of their stories. This separation is facilitated through an increase of mindfulness where the client is encouraged to see the difference between what he or she is experiencing as a problem and his or her power to choose to act differently toward the problem.

Films may provide a platform where the separation of the person's problem may be examined by distinguishing between the actor and the observer. Clients' perceptual, cognitive, behavioral, and emotional experiences learned from the past may limit, distort, and constrict their phenomenological access to the present moment. Therefore, they may be emotionally or cognitively blocked to see any other alternative way of looking at the stories they have lived through.

Langerian mindfulness brings a shift of attention where clients can get out of their socially and culturally constructed worlds and look for modes that may have been easily unnoticed. When people are mindlessly drowned into accepting their stories' unchangeability, they abide by the frequently repeated discourse of the same stories.

Practicing mindfulness allows people to realize that anxiety and depression can be choices one may accept. Deep down, the foundational prerequisites of the mindful management of depression and anxiety lie the power of choices.

One way to facilitate the shift of attention for exploring the possibility of multifarious layers and features in a film can transpire through watching and examining films. Films can provide a rich platform through which one may come to realize the changeability of the film's plot. In its broadest sense, art can also provide a significant medium where the observer may become mindful of the constructional nature of his or her mode of living through the power of words, images, and discourse (see Langer, 2009).

In line with the value of understanding the textual and subtextual configuration of films, Langerian mindfulness highlights the deconstruction of

Films and Mindfulness 27

a film's vitality. When people fail to express their lived stories or they are prevented from expressing their stories, or they are surrounded by people who insist on adopting a pretentious stance instead of relating and connecting to their stories, stories appear to operate in a wide variety of infiltrating and indirect contexts: Unexpressed stories do not cease to operate; they appear in different levels of one's intrapersonal and interpersonal relationships. A film is also representative of a form of a story. Its plot seems to be unchangeable since it is portrayed as the version of reality, but going back to the threads of the story demonstrates the power of changing it. For instance, when watching a film, the client can be encouraged to see what could have happened otherwise. What point in the story could have changed and brought a shift in action? What were the pieces in the film where the agency or the power of making a choice could be delineated?

Langerian mindfulness underlines the role of therapists in nonjudgmental, open, and flexible listening to help clients to freely and comfortably express their lived stories. This is also associated with the therapist's attunement and intersubjectivity and mindful presence, where he or she helps the client experience a sense of empathy, support, and flexibility in his or her therapeutic relationships. Empathy can be underlined through a reference to movies that facilitate the process of seeing the difference between two different psychological worlds. *A Christmas Carol* (2009) exemplifies a movie where this mood change and perspective plus cognition would happen.

Along with the review of a film's content and the experiential presence in therapeutic relationships, clients are encouraged to step outside the experience and observe their lived stories. This often happens through a combination of open questions where clients are invited to examine and realize how their own stories can be deconstructed into elements and features. The questions can first address the films and then go back to the clients' own stories.

Through this mindful deconstruction and decomposition, clients are encouraged to describe the experience and see how that description may have an impact on their feelings and behaviors. The bottom line here is to help clients understand the problem's externalization: They are not the problem; the problem is separate from them. Through an increase of mindfulness, clients learn to see how mindlessness may have contributed to identifying themselves with the problem. This may also take place through the therapist's explication of the role of internal vs. external attribution. An in-depth understanding of attribution's role would help clients realize how their mindsets may impose a relationship where change is not possible.

Mindfulness helps clients to break themselves free from the problem and realize their power of control, sensibility, choice, and power in creating a new meaning, a new story for themselves. This may happen through reflecting on a film and paying attention to its content, form, and discourse where the act of noticing can turn out to be an art in which the observer

28   *Films and Mindfulness*

makes a discernment of his or her novelty in paying attention to multiple potential layers of a story.

The Miracle Worker (1962) is a good example where the film elucidates the power of choice and agency in creating what seems impossible. Films can change the spectrum and sensibility of possibility.

The psychology of possibility is one of the conspicuous landmarks of the shift in Langerian mindfulness. The psychology of possibility offers a shift from "knowing what is" to "knowing what can be" (Langer, 2009, p. 15). The psychology of possibility critically questions the sovereignty and subjugation of knowing; it strikingly shatters the reliance on the structural repose of habitual ways of thinking; it ruptures the dependency on the plethora of circumscribing factors, including our thoughts, our experiences, our schemas, and our assimilating concepts. The psychology of possibility harbors the flight from the routinized discourse of entanglement within the prescribed signifiers to the infinite realm of becoming.

The psychology of possibility is not a positivist-driven psychology with a concentration on logical positivism, linear modes of thinking, and illness models. The psychology of mindfulness is a psychology of hope, faith, and meaning making; it is a psychology of self-empowerment, self-growth, and self-consummation. The psychology of possibility does not lie in negation and disconnectedness; it is a psychology of connectedness: it illustrates the possibility of repositioning one's self through a nonevaluative process in which negativity does not stop the process of furthering one's movement.

The psychology of possibility celebrates the process of becoming through a mindful examination of choices. The psychology of possibility allows one to linger in the spaces of being and becoming. The psychology of possibility highlights how our mindsets are paralyzed within the illusion of stability; the psychology of possibility enlightens the possibility of an exquisitely fresh experience with revitalizing implications. In elucidating this, Langer (2009) indicated that "we hold things still in our minds, despite the fact that all the while they are changing. If we open up our minds, a world of possibility presents itself" (p. 18). The psychology of possibility does not look for endorsement through probabilities; it encourages thinking beyond the stability of the established patterns of thinking. In dissociating from the dependency of mindset based on a mere focus on what "is" rather than what "can be," Langer (2009) wrote:

> There are many cynics out there who are entrenched in their beliefs and hold dear their view of the world as fixed and predictable. There are also people who, while not cynical, are still mindlessly accepting of these views. A new approach to psychology and our lives is needed because the naysayers—those who demand empirical evidence are—winning. It is they who have determined what's possible and what's achievable, to our collective detriment.

(p. 18)

Films and Mindfulness 29

Langerism may serve as a preamble for a transcendental process of being and becoming away from the quotidian engagements that only resonate with the entanglement's platitudes with the ordinary. In describing the possibility of such a process and its experiential understanding,
James (2002) wrote:

> There are possibilities [in us] that take our breath away of another kind of happiness and power based on giving up our own will and letting something higher work for us, and these seem to show a world wider than either physics or philistine ethics can imagine. Here is a world in which all is well.
>
> (p. 266)

In terms of applying mindfulness in watching films, one needs to realize that opening up the possibility in light of mindfulness may suggest the deliberate attempt to broaden the perspective. This may also require intentional flexibility to welcome new categories, new horizons of being and becoming, novel arenas of sensibility, and fresh avenues of exploration. This may usually be discouraged as entrapment by categories that incarcerate the likelihood of going beyond the predefined borderlines of validity, sensibility, and plausibility. The clients here can be invited to explore and examine different existing aspects in a film, features that may not be pervasive and can be easily ignored.

From a mindful perspective, the person looks into options in a wide variety of possibilities. There are huge practical differences of action. In the mindless scenario, the person is emotionally compelled through his or her mindlessness to be stuck in the inability of action; thus, there is no ability to respond in novel ways. In the mindful scenario, the person goes beyond this mindset and explores possible modes of controlling and influencing the situation.

This process of delving into the differences and shifts of attention may be feasible through watching the chain of events in a film and paying attention to its unfolding characteristics: As you watch a film, the movies starts opening up more of its essence and substance while providing the audience with ups and downs in emotional and cognitive realms. Depending on the genre, this textual manifestation occurs differently in terms of form, speed, and content. For instance, in movies with a suspense-oriented predilection, the opening is not at the same speed as that of movies with other genres.

Mindlessness paralyzes people's power of searching for otherwise in their stories (Fatemi, 2018). Mindlessness imposes a tunnel vision where the person is placed only in a circumscribing mode where possibilities are denied. This denial maximizes the negativity, weak points, and problems in the person's life while ignoring, marginalizing, and neglecting his or her strengths. Langerian mindfulness facilitates the process of finding the dominant stories and their discourses and their power to dictate the

30 *Films and Mindfulness*

impossibility of change and the certainty of the person's identification with the problem situations.

The dialectical journey of noticing new aspects of one's life along with attention to variability allows clients to see how their stories can be changeable: There are dimensions, features, and aspects in a film or a story that may not have been taken into consideration due to the heavy deluge of negatively induced mindlessness. *Brain on Fire* (2016) exemplifies a movie where most physicians move merely within their own perspective and are not readily prone to look at any other perspective.

Silence (2016) offers another example where sticking to one's certainty of knowing would give rise to catastrophic consequences. Films may be a great avenue for displaying how the dogmatic insistence on one's mindlessness and its interpretation as knowing may cost people irreparable damage and negative consequences.

When depressed, people may be mindlessly and automatically embedded within the negative repertoire of their recollection, associations, etc. Langerian mindfulness helps clients examine the bright side of their lives without denying the dark side.

So, for a depressed person, the questions would be are there times in your life where you have not experienced what you are experiencing now? What does that suggest? If you have not always been at the mercy of what you are now, does that not suggest that the experience is not equated with you: you are not what you experience? The goal is to help clients understand how mindlessness leads people to equate themselves with their mindsets and thus lose their power of choice.

By helping clients explore novel aspects of their situation by watching relevant films, Langerian mindfulness invites clients to extend their quest to locate positive sides in their own stories. Deconstructing the dominant-negative stories, their negative predilections, and their effects helps clients understand that they can re-author their own story through implementing mindful creativity in constructing a new horizon of possibility.

Helping clients in action to see the differences between mindlessness and mindfulness and their praxis in giving rise to different modes of realities in specifically selected films would serve as a preamble in illustrating the relationship between one's story and one's perspective.

Language plays a vital role in creating Langerian mindfulness. Langerian mindfulness helps clients be vigilant of the language they can mindfully use and its perlocutionary impacts. Language may imprison or emancipate people as it can revitalize or paralyze people's power of choice.

This understanding can take place with films that demonstrate how a change in language or the use of specific language may lead to constructions of different forms of realities.

My Fair Lady (1964), *The Sound of Music* (1965), *The Wolf of Wall Street* (2013), and *Hacksaw Ridge* (2016) are among both classic and

Films and Mindfulness 31

recent movies that entail the power of language in constricting or constructing realities.

A phenomenologically based experiential openness toward films and their manifestations or a practical connectedness to films may help people observe the subtle and rigorous impact of language in creating, shaping, transforming, and recreating realities. The discovery of one's voice, its power, and its impact unfolds itself in the process of a mindful therapeutic conversation.

The medium for leading the attention toward the process may vary from a focus on traditionally articulated films in the collective consciousness where attention to different layers would espouse finding something fresh in the context of those films, or it can be exemplified in accessing or activating different postmodern movies. The latter may also open up the interactive process of the "I" as the agent and "I" as the actor in the dialectically opulent rich relationships of emergent mindfulness.

With an abundantly experiential exposure to a mindful examination of one's agency, the power of choices may transpire in the diachronic and synchronic observation of one's own narratives. The generative sagacity of the process may contribute to the power to recompose one's narrative with composure and equanimity.

The following points and questions can be taken into consideration in applying mindfulness in films as a therapeutic mean:

1 When watching a film, clients can be asked to enlist the number of perspectives and their underlying emotional and cognitive components. In *12 Angry Men* (1957), for instance, clients can be invited to pay attention to all of the members' perspectives and examine how each perspective may bring about a different approach toward life and decision making.
2 Clients may be asked to watch a film and see how one event may be perceived from different angles. In *Prince and The Pauper* (1937), clients can learn how a choice-oriented detachment from one's own perspective and an attempt to near another possible perspective may help one lessen the phenomenological distance. In the meantime, clients may be encouraged to see how any given perspective may limit or constrict the possibility of an action or a decision. In *Guess Who's Coming to Dinner* (1967), the entrapment in one's perspective may not allow one to see the legitimacy of others' rights, feelings, emotions, sensibility, and even being.
3 Clients may be asked to watch a film and notice new things in addition to the obvious features of the film. Here, clients are inspired to leap beyond the film's appearance and look for novelty or exquisite facets of a film. This may lead to not only applying the analytical and synthetical competencies of the intellect but also to a process of emerging moments of the serendipitous discovery. In *Casbah* (1948),

for example, the film operates in numerous interwoven stages of creativity. On one level, it presages the story of insurgence, objection, and unorthodox behavior. On another level, it touches upon the tacit delicacy in the human spirit on the brink of inner conflicts. Increasing the attention level toward the multiplicities of meanings and perspectives would help clients increase their critical thinking, metacognition, mindfulness, and role sensitivity.

4   Clients may be invited to see how contexts can make a big difference in creating special context-bound meanings. From a mindful perspective, nothing is context free. Everything is bound by its context. The context may include emotional, cognitive, behavioral, social, political, and cultural spheres where the action or the event occurs. *I Confess* (1953) may be examined as an example where attention or inattention toward context would espouse contradictory analyses. *Scarlet Street* (1945), *Midnight in Paris* (2011), *Awakenings* (1990), *I Am a Fugitive From a Chain Gang* (1932), *Lost in Translation* (2003), and *Night on Earth* (1991) are among examples that point out the significance of contexts in creating meanings.

5   Films may serve as a vital medium to develop global mindfulness and heartful mindfulness. Clients can be encouraged to watch movies that touch upon macro or micro issues in life that can posit the

I Am a Fugitive From a Chain Gang (1932).

transformation of consciousness. These classes of films may bring about an enlightenment and illumination that signify the impact of emotions, actions, feelings, behaviors, cognitions, perceptions, and beings in a general and broader perspective. *Rosetta* (1999), *Cathy Come Home* (1966), *The Day After Tomorrow* (2004), *Selma* (2014), and *A Separation* (2011) may be considered in developing higher levels of mindfulness on global, human, and social issues.

6 Clients can be taught to see how relationships can go mindless through watching films that demonstrate the relationship between mindlessness and mindfulness. The relationship here includes both inner and interpersonal relationships: Cat *on a Hot Tin Roof* (1958), *Crazy Love* (2007), *Kramer vs. Kramer* (1979), *Modern Romance* (2017), *Scenes From a Marriage* (1974), *The War of the Roses* (1989), *The Way We Were* (1973), and *Who's Afraid of Virginia Woolf* (1966) are included in the list of films that discuss the role of different forms of mindlessness in decaying a relationship.

7 Clients can be encouraged to reflect on the possibility of multiple perspectives in a film. This can be done on several levels. If couples watch a film or everyone in a family watches a movie, they may come up with different interpretations and analyses. They may each focus on specific parts of a film. The difference itself opens up the room for highlighting the significance of perception and perceptual differences in encountering a film. The difference may be examined from different vantage points: thinking and cognitive styles; people process information differently. Some may think in terms of words, some in terms of images, some may look at an object and see the whole, while others may concentrate on the parts. One of the reasons for problems in communication may go back to different cognitive styles. People's negotiations and communications may fail because of conflicts in their thinking styles. Mindfulness helps clients understand the flexibility toward apprehending someone's thinking styles. This does not suggest ruling out one's cognitive styles, but it underscores the possibility of an attempt to familiarize oneself with the world of the other. Movies such as *To Kill a Mockingbird* (1962), *The Apartment* (1960), *Guess Who's Coming to Dinner* (1967), *Night on Earth* (1991), and *12 Angry Men* (1957) may be discussed to elucidate the significance of thinking styles in action.

8 In discussing mindfulness, clients may be encouraged to discuss the shift of perspectives connected with a scene and its consequences. In *Madam X* (1994), for instance, clients may be asked to see what could have happened if the mother-in-law had paid attention to an alternative view instead of insisting on her own.

9 Choose one or two films and see how the film may represent examples of mindlessness or mindfulness in different situations.

34 *Films and Mindfulness*

10 Choose a scene from a film where the example of mindlessness may be discussed and discuss how a shift from mindless into mindfulness could have led the characters in an entirely different direction.

11 Select a film where one can see the example of acting from a single perspective and its embedded mindlessness. Contrastively speaking, demonstrate how multiple perspectives may bring a fusion of horizons in decision making, performance enhancement, or an interpretation. *12 Angry Men* (1957) may be used as an example.

12 Choose a film where one's daily engagements and routinized behaviors may impede the process of living in the moment proactively.

13 Choose a movie where insensitivity to context can bring about mindlessness. When mindful, people pay attention to context and contextual factors.

14 Choose a film where you may notice new things other than what has been delineated in the film. Discuss how the inclusion of novelty in your interpretation and analysis may give rise to exquisite perspectives.

4 Why and How Films Can Be Therapeutic

Films may serve as an educational medium to create awareness and enlighten hearts and minds. In other words, films are the epitome of a human beings' expanded emotions, feelings, behaviors, perceptions, distortions, thinking dysfunctions, cognitions, attitudes, and life in general. A film reveals a cynosure of signification where meanings are not bound by merely the verbatim and dialogue but also images, music, lighting, camera angles, and sound effects. Films entail a rich repertoire of resources with three foci: the verbal, the vocal, and the visual components.

The Verbal

The verbal facet of films encompasses the atomic analysis of dialogues: dictions, choice of words, parlance, and the discourse within a movie. Words may be selected in a movie and may be exposed to a psychological examination. The lexical configuration in films can undergo different levels of analysis, including the grammatical, semantic, pragmatic interpretation, with all of them having an overall psychological tone. Clients can be encouraged to have heightened awareness of the dialogue in a film. In *A*

A Beautiful Mind (2001).

DOI: 10.4324/9780429441431-4

36 *Why and How Films Can Be Therapeutic*

Beautiful Mind (2001), for instance, the imagined friend says: "Nothing's ever for sure, it's the only sure thing I know."

The focus on the verbal part may include the modes of expressiveness, the order of words, the use of active or passive voice, the use of pronouns and anaphors, the placement of adverbs and adjectives, the change of formal into informal language, the use of slang and colloquialisms, the emphasis on standard or nonstandard use of language, etc. Viewers may be invited to sharpen their attention to the choice of words in dialogues, their order, their manner of expressiveness, their implications and impacts, etc.

Dialogues of a film may be examined to reveal psychological themes and psychological categories. They can also be studied in terms of the impact that they create, the productive use, or the hazardous applications that they can have. Dialogues may be scrutinized for their educational, informative, motivational, and persuasive impacts. *Scent of a Woman* (1992) is rife with examples of motivational and persuasive modes of expressiveness, especially when the colonel goes to school and talks about Charlie in front of a big audience.

Here are examples of the verbal in different movies:

1 "Frankly, my dear, I don't give a damn." *Gone With the Wind* (1939)
2 "I'm going to make him an offer he can't refuse." *The Godfather* (1972)
3 "Toto, I've got a feeling we're not in Kansas anymore." *The Wizard of Oz* (1939). It is interesting to note that this line has been parodied by many different movies and television shows.
4 "Here's looking at you, kid." *Casablanca* (1942)
5 "Go ahead, make my day." *Sudden Impact* (1983)
6 "You talking to me?" *Taxi Driver* (1976)
7 "I love the smell of napalm in the morning." *Apocalypse Now* (1979)
8 "Love means never having to say you're sorry." *Love Story* (1970)
9 "Rosebud." *Citizen Kane* (1941)
10 "When one door of happiness closes, another opens; but often we look so long at the closed door that we do not see the one which has been opened for us." *Hellen Keller* (1920)
11 "I would rather walk with a friend in the dark than alone in the light." *Hellen Keller* (1920)

In *Love in the Afternoon* (1957), for example, the order of the words at the end of the movie and its evocative sensations and associations may be examined with regard to the preceding pieces of the film and as catalysts to stimulate the episodic memory.

In *Compulsion* (1959), the verbatim enunciated by Orson Wells as a lawyer while stepping out of the courtroom may demonstrate the dialectical significance of a belief in a transcendental ontological perspective and

Compulsion (1959).

its implications for one's life. The short conversation between him and two clients sentenced to life imprisonment may highlight the creational capability of language in constructing and deconstructing assumptions.

Clients may be asked to ponder the use of words and the existing dialogues in films for different purposes—sometimes for modeling, sometimes for the impact of words in creating realities, and so forth. For instance, in *Citizen Kane* (1941), the urban slang "Rosebud" may reveal different denotative and connotative layers of meanings.

The Vocal

The vocal aspect in a film may include pitch, tone, pronunciation, enunciation, rhyme, rhythm, etc. A film may be analyzed on the strength of a psychological examination of these elements and their psychological implications, meanings, and roles in reinforcing, constricting, limiting, minimizing, and maximizing the saying in a film.

Obviously, the categories or their subdivisions may be scrutinized in a scene, sequential intervals, or the film's overall presentation.

The voice itself is subsumed under the vocal component. How the voice is articulated, expressed, and demonstrated is of significance here. The vocal analysis may also entail the presence of empowerment, disempowerment, helplessness, resourcefulness, fragility, briskness, or other features that might as well be conceived in the contextual film analysis.

For example, In *Forest Gump* (1994), the articulation of the words and the delicacy in the tone in his voice may accentuate kindness, simplicity, a childlike world, and humbleness.

Also, in *The Lion King* (2019), the voices of Scar and Mufasa hold many underlying and unexpressed messages that can be deciphered through the medium of tone. One may discern special strength, stature, and empowerment in Mufasa's voice and cowardice and pretentiousness in Scar's voice.

Forest Gump (1994).

The music can also be discussed and examined in line with the psychological analysis of the vocal component. For instance, the music played in *Psycho* (1960) has a huge psychological impact in intensifying the climate of petrification, fear, and terror.

The tone may display a wide variety of psychological positions. For example, in the beginning scene of the movie *Shawshank Redemption* (1994), when prisoners are taken to the prison yard, the officer in charge who welcomes the prisoner sends out a tone associated with hubris, dominance, and condescension. The final scene and the final tone in *I Am a Fugitive From the Chain Gang* (1932) portray fear, anxiety, trepidation, and petrification.

Citizen Kane (1941) portrays the human internal world and its connection to the external reality through a powerful demonstration of feelings and affects, emotions, and reactions. The rise and fall of feelings are vividly represented in the pitch and tone as the movie unfolds its power of creating surprises. Paying attention to the enunciation of "Rosebud" is an example to delineate the power of locutionary acts in displaying feelings.

Examination of the vocal components, including pitch, volume, pace, rhythm, rate, intonation, enunciation, pronunciation, accentuation, accentuation, etc., may demonstrate how a change in the manner of articulation or sound production may have an impact on producing different psychological effects.

To exemplify, the analysis of the specific emphasis on "That's quite a dress ..." in the movie *An American in Paris* (1951) may reveal how a change of stress from the word "quite" to the word "dress" may produce a different meaning.

Correspondingly, if the emphasis from the verb "play" is taken off and be placed on "Sam" in *Casablanca* (1942) in the following sentences, the whole meaning might change.

I Am a Fugitive From the Chain Gang (1932).

ILSA: Play it once Sam, for old time's sake.
SAM: I don't know what you mean, Miss Ilsa.
ILSA: Play it, Sam. Play "As Time Goes By."

Understanding and exploring the film's vocal components may demonstrate the interplay of the surface meaning and structural meanings. How the words are articulated can affect the perlocutionary impact.

The Visual

The visual facet of a film contains the objective and perceptible aspects of a film, such as proximity, spaces, makeup, ambiance, décor, facial expressions of actors and actresses, eye contact, body movement, posture, images, music, lighting, camera angles, etc.

How the camera zooms, the general appearance, colors, light, cinematography, special effects, the specific modes of the environmental presentation, and the image, in general, are all subsumed under the visual component.

In discussing a film's psychological analysis, one may highlight the importance or the relation, impact, and implications of such features in producing a psychological effect or giving rise to a specific psychological concept.

40 *Why and How Films Can Be Therapeutic*

Our focus on the visual component may also include the significance of the visual component in a context to bring symmetry, synergy, or dissonance in a scene.

In *Citizen Kane* (1941), for example, the use of deep-focus cinematography to display all objects in a shot in sharp detail or the film's look with low-angle shots and multiple points of view may be psychologically examined to elaborate the relationship between the specific techniques and their psychological implications.

The analysis of each of the components mentioned above in a film may broaden the understanding of the film's concepts, content, effects, etc. In addition, it helps clients to expand their perspective in real-life situations through focusing on communication patterns, listening skills, problem-solving skills, negotiation skills, etc. In other words, therapists may encourage clients to take note of the dialogue and the vocal and the visual parts of the film and see how each of those components may help them notice that they have not seen before. This opens up the possibility of delving into the interactions of human beings from multiple perspectives.

The following quotes from the movie *Hacksaw Ridge* (2016) may demonstrate how attitudes differ in dealing with a situation.

TOM DOSS: Did you figure this war is just going to fit in with your ideas?
DESMOND T. DOSS: While everybody is taking life, I'm going to be saving it, and that's going to be my way to serve.

The focus on war and life and their oppositional implications, the examination of life revitalization, and the general thematic coverage of life may open up a discussion on the ontological facets of life, the question of life, the meaning of life, and practical ways to deal with life in different lived situations. *Hacksaw Ridge* (2016) can thus be used as an example to present discussions on the phenomenology of life and war, one's resilience in difficult situations, and the emergence of meaning in catastrophic situations.

The following sentence from *Glengarry Glen Ross* (1992) is a clear example of a conversation suffused in consumerism, materialism, and utilitarianism. The movie and the following sentence, in particular, demonstrate how human identity may be merely interpreted through possessiveness and paraphernalia.

That watch costs more than your car. I made $970,000 last year. How much you make? You see, pal, that's who I am, and you're nothing. Nice guy, I don't give a shit.

Glengarry Glen Ross (1992) may highlight the critique of consumerism, materialism, and utilitarianism through a film that depicts how human indulgence in one's parochialism may overshadow one's access to wisdom.

Why and How Films Can Be Therapeutic 41

The film exemplifies the dog-eat-dog mentality and shows how egoism coupled with hubris and greed may devastate psychological well-being.

By focusing on the three significant facets of a film, namely, the verbal, the vocal, and the visual, therapists can lead the discussions to enlightening moments of self-awareness, self-management, social awareness, etc.

The following questions and suggestions may be used to facilitate the process of helping clients understand the practical applications of the three mentioned components:

1 When you watch a given film, make a list of the dialogues that are important to you and explain their relevance to your life and your situation.
2 What is it in the film that may be of significance to you in terms of the tone? What message does it have for you? How does that attention help you become more competent in communicating what you plan to do? Practice the example for your situation and pay attention to what happens when you experience a shift in tone and pitch.
3 Are there any specific features like an image or a space in the film that attracts your attention? What is it about the visual part that is important to you?
4 Are there any diction, words, or style of speech that you find constructive and helpful in improving your communication?
5 From what you see and hear, are there any aspects that could have been changed to improve the film's status? Choose a piece in the given film and show it could have been made differently.
6 If you were to redo the film, what would you change?
7 If you see yourself as the director of your own film and plan to recompose or decompose your own film, namely, your own story and your own life, what would you do? What would you add? What would you remove?
8 In view of considering films as texts, choose a movie of your own and discuss surface and structural meanings, core meanings, associative meanings, and marginal meanings.
9 Choose a film of your own and explore how meanings may be made in relationships, interactions, and transactions and classify the levels of cognitive, emotional, affective, and social meanings as they appear in the context of relationships.
10 Discuss how specific elements of a film, such as vocal or visual, may dominate the film and develop a discourse of their own.
11 Choose two films where you can identify the contrastive analysis of different discourses, such as the discourse of kindness versus the discourse of brutality.
12 Discuss the power of persuasiveness or motivation in specific films and demonstrate how the combination of vocal, verbal, and visual parts may add further strength and serve as complementary.

42 *Why and How Films Can Be Therapeutic*

13 Search for a movie where specific dialogues and scenes may reveal the inconsistencies between the verbal and the visual or the vocal and the verbal.

14 Choose a movie of your own interest and see how life paradoxes can be placed together in an interconnected chain of sensibility. Change can be selected as the core focus, for instance.

5 Films and Relationships

Relationships are an essential component of life. Everything goes back to relationships. We are born in relationships; we live through relationships, we continue our being and becoming through relationships. All of our mishaps or happiness, our failures or our success, our calamities or our prosperities occur in relationships. Films present and represent different modes of relationships as they illustrate the underlying elements of relationships.

Relationships unfold their dynamics, their ups and downs, their constructiveness, and their destructiveness in films. Films mirror relationships' failures, their successes, and their complexities. In films, one may see the dance of relationships and its cascades of movements. The enrichment or poverty of relationships is pictured in films.

An in-depth psychological analysis of relationships in films can go through several layers: the surface layer where we can see the perceptible and the obviousness of what appears to be happening in front of our eyes and the deep layer where the intricacies of relationships in different domains, including the conscious, preconscious, and unconscious may transpire or the cultural and local contexts of relationships may be revealed.

For instance, in the movie *Night on Earth* (1991), we can see the stories of different cab drivers in different cities of the world, with each having their unique narratives of belongings, longings, and sufferings. They each have their own discourse of communication, relatedness, and interactions. On the one hand, all of these taxi drivers have similarities and commonalities with one another, but each of them has their own placement and embeddedness in their culturally and locally constructed worlds.

Their responses and their reactions take place in their milieu of emotional, cognitive, and social contexts. The film demonstrates how each relationship may be subjected to an atomic analysis of the psychological components, including affect, emotion, memory, motive, cognition, etc. *Night on Earth* (1991) may point out the importance of understanding the grammar of relationships and its implications in accessing the local context. In the Rome episode where the cab driver picks up a clergyman, there are pouring instances of paradoxes in the dynamics of meaning-making, relatedness, and interactive responses. The episode is filled with the flow of

DOI: 10.4324/9780429441431-5

44 *Films and Relationships*

the paradoxes, from wearing dark glasses in the dark night to breaking the norms of societal conversation and going beyond the assumptions of ordinary folks in their daily engagements.

Some films may simply portray the contradictive relationships and conflicting interactions through presenting sequences and syntagmatic configurations that display the flagrant contraposition in relationships. In *Dial M for Murder* (1954), for instance, one does not need to be pensively curious to see the tension-oriented relationships in the characters as the film's façade and its continual focus may comfortably help the audience to grasp the traces of disturbed relationships.

In other films, one may see the subtlety of numerous flowing elements in relationships, whether interpersonal or intrapersonal. In *We're No Angels* (1989), for example, one may see the perfunctory aspect of the film in the prisoners who have escaped from prison and have been misidentified as priests. Interestingly, there are other layers of the film that depict the potentially available facets of relationships in everyone, including the transcendental and spiritual parts. In doing that, the film cogently pictures how the seeming outcasts can have piercing and deep relationships with foundational constituents of humanness. The movie challenges the sovereignty of appearance and ushers in the need to examine the unpretentiousness of human authenticity.

Films can show how relationships are subjected to sundry elements of consciousness. *Scarlet Street* (1945) may be cited as an example of a movie that demonstrates how one's relationship is under a barrage of so many

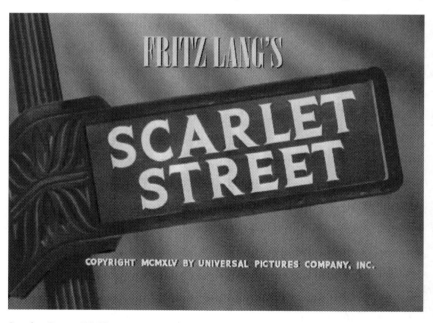

Scarlet Street (1945).

Films and Relationships   45

unpredictable factors. The movie depicts the relationship between the inner world and the external world as it portrays multidimensional jumps from the interpersonal reference points to the interpersonal realms.

The following examples of dialogue from the film may display the interconnectedness of relationships in different levels:

BANK EMPLOYEES: [*singing*] For he's a jolly good fellow. For he's a jolly good fellow. For he's a jolly good fellow, which nobody can deny, which nobody can deny, which nobody can deny, which nobody can deny.

JOHNNY PRINCE: Can't you get those Lazy Legs off that couch, baby?

JOHNNY PRINCE: And then you gave me a dirty look.

KITTY MARCH: I didn't give you a dirty look!

JOHNNY PRINCE: Listen, any girl that waits two hours in the rain for a guy is gonna give him a dirty look.

KITTY MARCH: Who do you think you are? My guardian angel?

MILLIE RAY: Not me, honey. I lost those wings a long time ago.

The movie examines how hidden unresolved conflicts in interpersonal and intrapersonal relationships may give rise to big and dramatic changes in one's behavior and responses.

Scarlet Street (1945) relates the story of a man who is engaged in his mundane world and is suddenly exposed to some emotional encounter that impacts his reactions to the world. He is overwhelmed by emotions and run over by his indulgence in the emotional world. His surrender to his emotionally controlled mind brings about his submission to the demands and desires of a woman who impersonates a character to merely manipulate him to do what she wants him to do. The movie touches upon manifold issues from love and conscience to theft, jealousy, murder, and confusion.

The movie may be discussed with clients regarding its rich repertoire of relationship's ups and downs, vulnerability, emotional dysregulation, reactivity and impulsivity, and mindlessness. It can be rigorously discussed in terms of its delineation of what happens when you are not aware of your emotions.

In discussing the relationships, clients can be asked to view the film and get a general sense of the plot, the story, and the vocal, verbal, and visual components. They are then asked to see how the relationships have failed or progressed and analyze the mode of development in each relationship. Clients are invited to examine the impact of emotional factors in giving rise to changes in relationships. They are asked to see how the intrapersonal or interpersonal factors have contributed to the development of relationships, construction, or devastation.

Relationships can be characterized through positive approaches and responses to needs, wants, and desires. In welcoming relationships, people's

46 *Films and Relationships*

needs, wants, and desires or concerns are taken seriously. They are welcome through positive responses, affection, and kind returns. When two people communicate in a welcoming relationship, each feels respected, loved, and taken care of, whereas in unwelcoming, aggressive, passive, abusive, manipulative, and poisonous relationships, the needs, wants, concerns, desires, rights, and perspectives of people in the relationship are disregarded, denied, trivialized, suppressed, disapproved of, and ignored.

Movies provide a suitable platform to display different modes of relationships and their impacts.

The following exchange of words in the movie *Who Is Afraid of Virginia Wolf* (1966) may depict a bitter and an unwelcoming relationship:

GEORGE: You're a monster—You are.

MARTHA: I'm loud, and I'm vulgar, and I wear the pants in the house because somebody's got to, but I am not a monster. I'm not.

The following from the movie *Revolutionary Road* (2008) present another example of a relationship fraught with disrespect, insult, and hatred:

APRIL WHEELER: What are you going to do now? Are you going to hit me? To show me how much you love me?

FRANK WHEELER: Don't worry, I can't be bothered! You're not worth the trouble it would take to hit you! You're not worth the powder it would take to blow you up. You are an empty, empty, hollow shell of a woman. I mean, what the hell are you doing in my house if you hate me so much? Why the hell are you married to me? What the hell are you doing carrying my child? I mean, why didn't you just get rid of it when you had the chance? Because listen to me, listen to me, I got news for you—I wish to God that you had!

Clients may be encouraged to look for signs of healthy or unhealthy communication. They may also be invited to reflect on the structural components of a relationship where the underlying elements of a relationship have already been decayed, ruined, and destroyed.

A rigorous analysis of a given movie focusing on relationship formation, relationship conflict, relationship dissolution, or relationship crises may highlight critical stages in a relationship where self-awareness, emotional awareness, relationship management, and problem-solving skills can play a vital role in reducing the risks in a relationship.

On a micro level, the relationship in a movie can be subjected to an atomic analysis where the visual, verbal, and vocal components of people in a relationship may be explored in terms of synergy, congruence, effectiveness, and impacts.

Movies such as *Modern Times* (1936), a classic Charlie Chaplin silent movie, and other movies including *The Graduate* (1967), *Bean* (1997),

The Graduate (1967).

American Psycho (2002), and *Drive* (2011) delineate the roles and functions of microscopic elements of a relationship. The elevator scene in *Drive* (2011), for instance, elucidates the power of nonverbal communication and its implications for creating meaning.

The movie *Splendor in the Grass* (1961) epitomizes the changing dance of relationships over time while including the lines of poetry from William Wordsworth in his poem called "Ode: Intimations of Immortality."

Therapists can select different movies with different aspects of relationships and ask clients to watch the selected films and find the movie's dominant themes in terms of relationships. Clients can then be asked to see if there are points or examples from the film that may apply to their own lives connected with similarities. In line with a mindful observation of the relationship's dynamics in the given films, clients are asked to look for signs of wellness, vulnerability, and well-being in the quality of relationships.

Examples of passive, aggressive, and assertive behaviors can be explored within the realm of relationships. Clients can be invited to see how a change from one style to another could have led the characters in a different direction. In *Splendor of the Grass* (1961), for example, clients can be invited to ponder the nature of relationships and see the role of the boy's father in escalating the tension in the relationship instead of creating calm. If the father had had a different attitude, how could the whole scenario have changed? Are there examples in the client's relationships where his or her inflexibility might give rise to similar consequences?

The following questions can be used in terms of discussing the importance of relationships in a movie:

1. What are the components of the dialogue in each interaction? What is it that they say? (verbal) How do they say that? (vocal) What is it that they show while they say something? (visual) *North by Northwest* (1959) may be discussed as an example to elucidate each of the elements.

48 *Films and Relationships*

2 Is there congruency among the modes of communication? Are there signs of incongruency? What is it that makes the interaction incongruent? *Dial M for Murder* (1954) may be exemplified in line with an in-depth look at communication modes.

3 What is the style of the interaction in each dialogue? Is there a dominant style throughout the movie? Are there signs of defensive, passive, aggressive, or assertive communication in the relationship?

4 *Who Is Afraid of Virginial Wolf* (1966) may be a good example of illustrating different forms of interactions with different modes.

5 Are there examples in the movie where silence can open a place for creating special meanings? *Silence* (2016) is a great example of demonstrating such a phenomenon at both micro and macro levels.

6 What are the examples of an interpretive lens through which the meaning is created? How does an interpretation change or influence a behavior? How is the meaning constructed through an interpretation? *Guess Who's Coming to Dinner* (1967) may instantiate how an interpretation may affect an interaction or a decision.

6 Films and Understanding

Films provide a multifarious medium for understanding. This includes cognitive, emotional, moral, cultural, social, and spiritual understandings. Understanding may also be examined on the strength of analyzing the perspective of the spectator or audience. For instance, Lacanian psychoanalysis may be used as an analytical approach focusing on the perspective of the camera, and it creates a gaze on the events of the film's narrative.

In similar domains, the analysis of characters in Freudian terms may provide a different level of understanding where one can go for the psychoanalytical understanding of characters in films. Another spectrum of understanding may entail understanding the underlying elements of techniques used by the filmmakers or screenwriters and cinematographers in general. A similar quest for understanding may unfold its concentration on psychoanalyzing unconscious mechanisms such as repression, splitting, condensation, displacement, and projection that may be accessible in a film's textual analysis.

Understanding the multifarious dimensions of a film may also indicate our curiosity for further understanding ourselves. From a cognitive perspective, understanding may take place at different levels. For instance, children experience higher levels of cognitive understanding as they grow. Children may not have a great understanding of a dialogue, a conversation, and its underlying elements at younger ages: they may look for action. Sound effects or certain motions and colors grab their attention. They have difficulty understanding how narratives work, how the plot is formed, and how stories are related to interconnected internal and external elements (see Meadowcroft & Reeves, 1989).

The same holds true for emotional understanding: With development, people experience higher levels of emotional understanding. A child cannot understand suspense in a movie at younger ages since he or she can focus only on distinctly individual constituents and not holistic and interconnected facets of a story.

The process of understanding may also be expanded with further development in moral, social, cultural, and spiritual domains. Lack of development in any of these areas may impede the process of understanding.

DOI: 10.4324/9780429441431-6

50 *Films and Understanding*

Along with the aforementioned modes of understanding, one may discuss other forms of understanding when watching a movie. Understanding may involve a deeper level of connection to the existing messages within a movie or discovering, exploring, searching, and analyzing what lies beyond the movie's surface.

So, the film here opens up different worlds and different horizons of discovery. At one level, it opens up what is manifested through the interaction of verbal, vocal, and visual elements on the surface. On another level, it unearths the other existing yet rigorous elements within the film's textual configuration. Thus, understanding is characterized by an intentional, attentive, open, flexible, mindful, and meticulous search for higher levels of meanings in a film.

Life of Pi (2012), *Amelie* (2001), *Life Is Beautiful* (1997), *A Christmas Carol* (1938), *Cast Away* (2000), *As It Is in Heaven* (2004), *Lucy* (2014), *Spring, Summer, Fall, Winter… and Spring* (2003), *Mr. Nobody* (2009), *American Dreams* (2006), *The Matrix* (1999), *Gandhi* (1982), and *Bajrangi Bhaijaan* (2015) may be classified among movies that potentiate myriad modes of understanding beyond the appearance of the surface layers of meanings.

Encouraging the search within the clandestinely available threads of meanings in a film would open up the sphere of understanding complex and complicated rays of connections at both micro and macro levels, in both intrapersonal and interpersonal domains. Films, in this sense, serve as a great tool for metacognition, mindfulness, meta-analysis, deep psychology, and transcendental understanding.

To understand a film, we need to go beyond the surface components and explore the rigorous layers of a film and its discourse, opening a new world. This understanding may also belong to inward factors, that go beyond semiotic level. In the book *Philosophical Grammar*, Wittgenstein (1974) introduces such a deep understanding. Wittgenstein describes a situation in which you receive a card from a loved one that says, "I arrive in Vienna on the 24th of December!" Wittgenstein describes the phenomenon in this way:

> They aren't mere words! Of course not: when I read them, various things happen inside me in addition to the perception of the words: maybe I feel joy, I have images, and so on. But I don't just mean that various more or less inessential concomitant phenomena occur in conjunction with the sentence; I mean that the sentence has a definite sense, and I perceive it. But then what is this definite sense? Well, that this particular person, whom I know, arrives at such and such a place, etc. Precisely: when you are giving the sense, you are moving around in the grammatical background of the sentence. You're looking at the various transformations and consequences of the sentence as laid out in advance, and so they are "laid out in advance," in so far as they are embodied in the grammar.
>
> (Wittgenstein, 1974, p. 153)

Films and Understanding 51

This understanding, which is embodied in the "grammatical background," does not consist in the intralinguistic or linguistic understanding. This understanding of films may unfold manifold levels: It partially depends on the linguistic environment at the intralinguistic level, so the viewer must be able to have essential familiarity with the assortment and configuration of semiotic signs in a particular language. More important than that, the understanding should occur in the grammatical background, namely, the conceptual background, which provides the integration of the meaning with our own experience so it would enable us to get connected to the semantics profoundly. This understanding is not solipsistic and subjectivist, nor is it a Romanticist one.

Films entail two distinct substances, namely, intralinguistic and extralinguistic ones. The intralinguistic constituents of films embody themselves in the semiotic entities or signs by which the story or narrative of a film is told or narrated in a particular linguistic system of a language. These constituents can be discussed and analyzed in light of a specific taxonomy of the particular semiotic entities within a distinctive semiotic system in a particular language. Here, we may single out and discuss distinct appearances of language in particular aspects such as syntax, phonology, morphology, etc. A film unavoidably unravels and discloses itself within some specific linguistic system, thus generating and producing special semiotic entities. We may look at the semiotic entities of a film and examine and identify specific constituents at an intralinguistic level. The following piece from the movie *Pride and Prejudice* (2005) may reveal the interplay of intralinguistic and interlinguistic levels.

ELIZABETH BENNET: I wonder who first discovered the power of poetry in driving away love.
MR. DARCY: I thought poetry was the food of love.
ELIZABETH BENNET: Of a fine, stout love it may. But if it is only a vague inclination, I'm convinced one poor sonnet would kill it stone dead.
MR. DARCY: So what do you recommend to encourage affection?
ELIZABETH BENNET: Dancing. Even if one's partner is barely tolerable.

Let us assume that we hear a sentence such as "I want to understand it" in a film that is essentially exteriorized in an assortment of sentences and clauses in a particular language. We may look at the intralinguistic constituents of the sentence and examine one or some aspects from a selective point of view within the intralinguistic systems of the language. For example, in the sentence "I want to understand it," mentioned above in our hypothetical case, we notice a split infinitive. A split infinitive is a structure in which "to" and the rest of the verb is separated by an adverb. Although a lot of people consider a split infinitive bad style, it is quite common in English, particularly in an informal style that may be frequently used in films. (The famous American writer Raymond Chandler

52 Films and Understanding

got very angry when his British publisher corrected his split infinitives. He wrote a letter saying, "When I split an infinitive, goddamn it, I split it, so it stays split.")

The intralinguistic components that were identified in our analysis make sense in a specific semiotic system, viz. the linguistic system of the English language. They do not make any sense in another language such as German, Arabic, French, Farsi, etc., since these constituents lie in the heart of their producing linguistic system in that they are enclosed within the system in which they were born.

In other words, the appearance of specific signs with specific characteristics within a specific linguistic system is only encased in the given linguistic system. It cannot happen in any other linguistic system. The phoneme p, for example (whether aspirated as in "pet" or nonaspirated such as in "spat") only occurs in the English phonological system, although there may be similar brothers and sisters for the same sign, say, in Persian language. Hence, the p in English is entirely different from p in Farsi or the Persian language.

In this sense, films cannot be transferred from one language into another language since they appear within semiotic signs of a linguistic system that makes sense only in that particular language.

The extralinguistic components of a film reveal the film's predilections, relations, representations, and revelations on extralinguistic realities. Here films display their presentation of things such as relations, passions, actions, state of affairs, events, positions, knowledge, existence, absence, etc.

The phenomena being disclosed in this stage of films produce propositions, statements, and enunciations that ontologically and epistemologically describe realities constructed in the narration of narratives in films.

The extralinguistic components of films can be transferred from one language into another language through translation. Here we encounter the component that cannot be encapsulated in circumscribed borders thanks to the complexity of the underlying constituents of films; that is, human complexity of action, state of mind, events, etc. For the same reason, we cannot formulate the happenings of films definitively, for each film is tantamount to a new birth of meaning in a semantic level, albeit old in the semiotic level.

Although productive attempts have been made to explore the patterns of transpiration and explain the quiddity of happenings and their form of occurrence in films such as the Aristotelian concept of plot or the typical five-act tragedy as described by the German critic Gustav Freytag as well as the relevant conceptual offshoots such as climax and denouement, one cannot invent the "what" and "how" of a film that has not yet been produced thanks to the unpredictable element of human involvement in the process of action within the narratives. Therefore, one cannot certainly say how a film will be made, although one may be able to partially explain

Films and Understanding 53

how the story of a film has occurred. In other words, any story within a film is characterized uniquely because of the exclusively complex human constituents that construct the semantics of the narrative beyond the familiar and identified ways.

So, although there are expressed ways that may be common to numerous narratives of films, each film has an unexpressed way compared to previously expressed narratives that are presented through its narration.

The extralinguistic substance of films also presents and represents a film's ontological perspective, so the extralinguistic component can display the existential and nonexistential categories within the films. Films also introduce knowing and ways of knowing on an epistemological level in that they report ways or sources through which knowing manifests itself. This may happen both explicitly or implicitly within the circulation, buoyancy, and construction of narratives.

Let's consider the following segment from the movie *The Life of Emile Zola* (1937) to see how the extralinguistic plays a role in a story.

EMILE ZOLA: To save Dreyfus, we had to challenge the might of those who dominate the world. It is not the swaggering militarists! They're not but puppets that dance as the strings are pulled. It is those others, those who would ruthlessly plunge us into the bloody abyss of war to protect their power. Think of it, Alexandrine, thousands of children sleeping tonight under the roots of Paris, Berlin, London. All the world! Doomed to die horribly under some titanic battlefield unless it can be prevented! And it can be prevented! The world must be conquered, but not by force of arms, but by ideas that liberate. Then can we build it anew, build for the humble and the wretched! That's good! I must remember that.

In addition to the presence of the semiotic units that have physically given rise to the production of the above, there can be an extralinguistic component in the above that, for example, acknowledges the ontology of ideas as a significant extension of the ontological taxonomy. One can also see the introduction of a new way of knowing amidst the semantic units of the above. The extralinguistic constituents of the above-cited segment of the film incorporate numerous entities such as the relation of the domineering pole in the world and their ploys in manipulating others, the concept of oppression and it's happening in various modes, the passion for liberation and the state of oppression, etc.

Films may also provide views with the possibility of different levels of understanding and misunderstandings. As the viewing may take place on the surface of the early emergent components of the film, namely, vocal, visual, and verbal facets of a film, the connection to understanding may transpire in simple or complex layers. At simple levels, one may only consider the hermeneutic interpretation of a film merely based on reductionist approaches.

54 *Films and Understanding*

Bajrangi Bhaijaan (2015).

One may discuss *Bajrangi Bhaijaan* (2015) in terms of the story, its plot, its narrative sequences, its perfunctory elements of light, its ambiance, its sounds, its colors, its effects, its diction, its discourse, and their signification and their sensibility in the movie. One may go beyond and address other questions such as:

1 What is it that makes a man accept harsh and adverse conditions to pursue his goal?
2 What is it that makes people so negligent and ignorant toward understanding their own actions? How does social pressure impose premature cognitive understanding in connection with one's perspective?
3 How can one resist the flux of conformity, social pressure, and the majority's power when it comes to maintaining one's values?
4 What is the role of social and emotional support from family members and friends when it comes to trials and sufferings?
5 What is the role of media in distorting realities?
6 How does one encounter one's choice of freedom amid hardships and encumbrances?
7 What brings about perseverance in the face of objections and oppositions?
8 What is the dialectics of delicacy and hardships: how does one move ahead with the images of beauty and glory in mind?
9 Can one see beauty while encountering the harshness of life?

The following points can be taken into consideration by therapists while focusing on understanding the films:

1 What are some obvious levels of understanding in the given film?
2 Are there specific sentences or images and scenes that may facilitate or highlight a level of understanding?

Films and Understanding 55

3 What are some of the manifest verbal and nonverbal aspects of the film that can be easily understood?

4 Do you see any link in the genre or the film's content that may help you better understand some of the concepts that we have discussed in our session?

5 Do you agree or disagree that this film has layers that can be easily understood by everyone? If yes, or no, why?

6 How do you see this film's role or other films that we have discussed in creating a novel understanding of ourselves, our relationships, and our challenges?

7 Are there specific pieces in the film that you think might require a grammar of understanding, as we elaborated in our session?

8 How do you see the distinction between a superficial understanding and a deep understanding of this film?

9 How do you see the distinction between what one may know or what one may understand in this film?

10 Do you see any relationship between this film and your own personal experience or your lived experiences?

7 Films and Development

When discussing development, it may conjure up the focus on cognitive, emotional, and moral development as examined in the developmental psychological texts.

Here development may be discussed in a related and yet distinct mode. Watching a film may provide an avenue for looking into the learning opportunities provided in the film and may have an impact on social and interpersonal relationships or, in broader contexts, bring about growth, development, and enhancement in sundry domains of life. This may include relationship development, personal development, emotional development, spiritual development, and intellectual development.

For instance, when watching a film such as *The Wolf of Wall Street* (2013), one may see how the film's content may produce thought-provoking topics in self-awareness, relationship management, and emotional management such as self-motivation. This might lead to asking questions

I Confess (1953).

DOI: 10.4324/9780429441431-7

Films and Development   57

such as: What is the leading compass in one's life? Is one subject to one's desires, or are there ways to manage the desires? Is this management an illusion or real? What are the roles of values in one's life? What are the implications of running a goal-oriented life versus a value-oriented life?

The movie *I Confess* (1953) presents a lively example of how one's values and one's life can be interconnected. Speaking up and defending oneself and prove someone wrong in the midst of hardships and encumbrances may be replaced with silence merely by abiding by the values one holds.

Movies can be exemplified in terms of their potential messages for growth and development: for breaking the habits of automaticity and searching for meaning and purpose, scrutinizing the possibility of thinking about thinking, reflecting on the power of choices, and understanding the role of awareness.

In *Mona Lisa Smile* (2003), for instance, the following diction may serve as a preamble for celebrating mindfulness and creativity:

KATHERINE WATSON: Look beyond the paint. Let us try to open our minds to a new idea.

Movies may also provide a platform for spiritual development and understanding. They can open up new paradigms of development and thinking. In the movie *The Wrong Man* (1956), a man is innocently accused of a crime that he did not committed. He does his best to prove his innocence. He hires lawyers, brings eyewitnesses, and does whatever he can in the material world. Nothing works. In the midst of his desperation and disillusionment, his mother suggests that he communicate with God. Right at the moment of his appeal and supplication, the real criminal is arrested. The movie tries to depict the power of prayer and its implications.

In discussing the power of spiritual development, George Vaillant (2008) indicated that

> Skeptical academic minds have tended not to accept the universal importance of spirituality in human life. Too often, the mere mention of spirituality leads academics to roll their eyes with the same disbelief—dare I say disgust—with which Skinner treated emotion. Academics have wished to keep scientific and spiritual truths separate, insisting that the scientific truth is truer than the spiritual. I believe that is a mistake. (p. 206)

Vaillant (2008) underscores the significance of development in connection with love and indicates that

> successful human development involves absorbing love; next, reciprocally sharing love; and, finally, giving love unselfishly away. All of the great religions, our friends, our families, our genes, and our brain

58 *Films and Development*

chemistry conspire to guide us along this path. Always love multiplies like "a magic penny." As Shakespeare's Romeo exclaims to Juliet, "My bounty is as boundless as the sea, my love as deep; the more I give to thee, the more I have, for both are infinite".

(p. 102)

No wonder some regard God and love as synonymous.

Movies may display the relation between self-development and relationship development.

The point is to illustrate that development is not just bound to one level or stage, such as intellectual and cognitive development. Movies may provide numerous examples of emotional and spiritual development, too.

The Song of Bernadette (1943) is a movie interspersed with multifarious aspects of meanings and potentially rich prompts to elucidate the significance of the possibility of development in one's life, one's character, one's perspective, and one's responses to world happenings.

The following quotes from the movie may be worth pondering in terms of content, perlocutionary impact, and locutionary and illocutionary effects:

PEYRAMALE: [*to Bernadette*] Wake up! Now! Else life is at an end for you. You are playing with fire, Bernadette.

DR. DOZOUS: There was something about her that precluded laughter. Her exaltation was so genuine that the observer almost had the impression that he saw what the child saw.

A therapeutic discussion on the aforementioned movie may open up space to discuss paradigms, epistemic domains, and contemplative practices.

A young French woman (Bernadette) experiences vivid visions of the Virgin Mary, and most people dismiss her claims. Some people, including the priest Dominique Peyramale, gradually believe her. Bernadette is ultimately found to be a saint. She becomes a nun at a convent and faces jealously and intolerance from seemingly religious people who cannot see Bernadette's status.

A discussion can revolve around so many topics, including the possibility of going beyond five senses, the likelihood of communication with the Divine, the sensibility and insensibility of the language of understanding for those immersed in the material world, and the implications of a new emergent paradigm where concepts and contents differ from the previously lived situation.

The movie can lead perception through the immensely opulent zones of reflexivity where one can sit back and watch one's being as both an observer and an actor.

The development discussed here encompasses various contexts, including intellectual, emotional, and spiritual development.

The argument is not aimed at claiming that merely watching a film would lead to development. But it tends to suggest that movies may

Films and Development 59

delineate different types of development from which one can get inspiration. *The Miracle Worker* (1962), focusing on Hellen Keller's story, is an example of a movie that demonstrates how possibility can be extended beyond the borders of ordinary discourse. It displays how love, support, and perseverance can give rise to different development forms that may not be imaginable through the regular eyes of reasoning, habituation, and computation.

The following quotes from Hellen Keller may be used and discussed in line with the examination of the types of developments in thoughts, feelings, and behaviors from the movie:

> When one door of happiness closes, another opens, but often we look so long at the closed door that we do not see the one which has been opened for us.

> The best and most beautiful things in the world cannot be seen or even touched. They must be felt with the heart.

Hellen Keller's words open a new horizon of understanding and go beyond the conventional parlance and paradigm of development. She elucidates the ontological expansion of mind and heart through liberation from the visible world's taken-for-granted postulations.

Her words call for revisiting our intrapersonal and interpersonal relationships for approaching the quiddity of life. The following words from Hellen Keller display her shift of paradigms from the world of actualities in the material realm:

> Death is no more than passing from one room into another. But there's a difference for me, you know. Because in that other room, I shall be able to see.

> Relationships are like Rome—difficult to start out, incredible during the prosperity of the golden age, and unbearable during the fall. Then, a new kingdom will come along, and the whole process will repeat itself until you come across a kingdom like Egypt that thrives and continues to flourish. This kingdom will become your best friend, your soul mate, and your love.

In discussing and examining the role of development in movies and their therapeutic or educational implications, one may address or focus on the following questions:

1 What is it in the movies that goes beyond the automatic behavior and demonstrates an attempt to demonstrate proactive and mindfulness behavior?

60 *Films and Development*

2 How does the transition from automaticity to mindfulness occur?

3 How does a search for meaning and purpose contribute to a new understanding of oneself and one's life?

4 What is the role of a value-oriented life in achieving a higher level of emotional development?

5 How does one's indulgence in habitual and mundane realities of daily life prevent one from an integrated focus on one's development?

6 How does the given movie help one revisit one's process of relationship development?

7 How does the given movie bring about a new perspective in revitalizing one's development?

8 What is the significance of the role of *the other* or *the Other* in hampering or facilitating the process of development? For instance, *I Am a Fugitive From a Chain Gang* (1932), *Vice* (2018), and *The Hurricane* (1999) explicate instances of how *the other* and *the Other* stop the process of one's development in numerous areas of emotional, social, intellectual, relationship, intrapersonal, and spiritual development.

9 How does one overcome the impediments of development? What are the roles of hope, faith, and prayer in improving or implementing one's development? *The Wrong Man* (1956), *Gandhi* (1982), and *The Message* (1976) may be examined in terms of their power in giving rise to challenging obstructions against social, individual, and spiritual development.

10 How does an understanding of emotional management occur in connection with watching a movie, and what are the implications of exploring the possibility of human development?

8 Films and Emotion

Films are filled with emotions and emotional messages. You can rarely find a movie where emotions are not highlighted. Movies are replete with emotional tones and emotional illustrations, including positive and negative emotions. Some films are so strong in eliciting emotional messages that right at the beginning of the movie, the barrage of emotions marshal their forcible presence and overwhelm the audience with their impact.

The Reader (2008), *Fish Tank* (2009), *Requiem for a Dream* (2000), *Wings of Desire* (1987), *Moonlight* (2016), *Inside Out* (2015), *and Cast Away* (2000) may fall into the category where emotional messages are rampantly available.

Emotions are vital for understanding human life, and emotional awareness is a leading component of well-being (see, for instance, Schnall & Roper, 2011; Silvers & Haidt, 2008).

Cast Away (2000).

DOI: 10.4324/9780429441431-8

62 Films and Emotion

Clients can be encouraged to watch movies and examine how positive and negative emotions are displayed and expressed both nonverbally and verbally. This can include a discussion of emotions and their implications for personal and social relationships. It may also cover the extension of emotions on larger scales. The focus may entail the effects of those emotions on the viewer. Wedding and Niemiec (2014) discussed and presented examples of emotional elevation in movies where viewers experience a positive state of emotion and experience inspirations to proceed with positive actions, including prosocial behavior.

Clients can also be encouraged to watch given films and discuss whether they can find examples where emotions are managing one's actions or one is able to manage one's emotions. Clients can also be encouraged to search for examples of empathy in movies and how they are expressed and displayed.

Searching for emotional demonstration may also provide viewers with the possibility of understanding the power of agency and choice in dealing with emotional manifestation.

In other words, is the person solely condemned by his or her emotions, or can he or she have a choice to deal with those emotions? What is it in the emotional barrage that stops one from operating from the position of agency instead of automaticity?

As much as an in-depth excavation of the multifarious layers of an emotional performance may allow us to detect and acknowledge the interconnectedness of an array of possible variables in shaping the specificity of the emotion-oriented performance, one may set out to delve into the implications of agency and choice as the creative force of the performer in giving rise to his or her performance. This may apply to different forms of dual-process theories, including the computer model of serial information processing and the neural network model of parallel information processing.

The former assumes that only one form of thinking can occur at a certain time, so they rule out the possibility of a simultaneous form of both effortful and effortless thinking, whereas the latter claims the possibility of the simultaneousness of two types of parallel thinking (see Epley et al., 2002; Kahneman & Frederick, 2002).

In other words, we may let our analysis concentrate on the performing agent's status in producing the outcome, namely, the performance within a specific domain. This will be ineluctably tied to perceptive attention to both the process and the outcome as they are mutually linked to the etiological configuration of agency as the cause behind the performance.

A rigorous scrutiny of the psychological status of an agency may help us notice how the agency unfolds itself in the production of a special form of an emotion-oriented performance.

As we reflect on the role of agency in structuring and shaping the quiddity of performance, we may ponder the significance of such questions:

Films and Emotion 63

1   Is the agency fully functioning as it facilitates the process of an emerging performance: is an agent behind the power of agency quintessentially connected to the creative process of a performance, or is he or she half-engaged in producing his or her performance?

2   How can the power of agency enhance the efficacy of a performance? Are there ways to help an actor behind an agency to increase his or her power of agency?

Back to our previous discussions on mindfulness, we may find it worthwhile here to see the relationship between mindfulness and emotionally induced performance.

The foundational experiments of Langer and Rodin (1976) and the contrast analysis found in the studies of Schulz (1976; Schulz & Brenner, 1977; Schulz & Hanusa, 1978, 1979; Schulz & Heckhausen, 1996, 1997; Schulz et al., 1991, 1999) demonstrate a number of substantive points within Langerian mindfulness.

Langerian mindfulness focuses on the agency as the main component of mindfulness in that the actor relies on his or her own agency as the initiator of the action; thus, the initiation takes place from an inward source.

In Langer and Rodin's study (1976), the residents in the nursing home realized that the action was theirs and that they needed to take it upon themselves to proceed with that. In Schulz's experiment (1976; Schulz & Brenner, 1977; Schulz & Hanusa, 1978, 1979; Schulz & Heckhausen, 1996, 1997; Schulz et al., 1991, 1999), the residents were exposed to the contingency of agency: They were dependent on the initiation of action from outside, from the student aides who determined the timing of their social interactions. The residents had to wait for external factors to manifest themselves in the body of the agency.

Langerian mindfulness with a focus on agency highlights the possibility of the implementation of agency through expanding the horizons of action: The actor discerns that the mindset of impossibility lies as one perspective out of many; a change of perspective opens up the possibility of exploring possible alternative modes of action. The change happens through activating one's power of agency to explore new horizons of possibility. The actor does not succumb to the fixation of the apparent impossibility. The residents in the nursing home in Langer and Rodin's experiment (1976) came to realize that mindset can be changed. The mindset of hopelessness and helplessness was simply a choice, and they could experience a shift of mindset through celebrating multiple perspectives. The possibility of the shift was induced by underscoring the significance of a change from the perspective of passivity to the perspective of responsibility. The ability to respond through one's own agency stood at the top of the initiation. In Schulz's experiment (1976; Schulz & Brenner, 1977; Schulz & Hanusa, 1978, 1979; Schulz & Heckhausen, 1996, 1997; Schulz et al., 1991, 1999), the residents experienced the possibility of

64 *Films and Emotion*

change through the action of others, so the agency was other oriented: it was dependent on the initiation of others' agency.

The phenomenological aspect of control may explain why and how Langer and Rodin's (1976) induced control group, who received a message based on an enduring sense of control, acted differently than Schulz's group (1976; Schulz & Brenner, 1977; Schulz & Hanusa, 1978, 1979; Schulz & Heckhausen, 1996, 1997; Schulz et al., 1991, 1999), for whom the sense of control was temporary. Phenomenology discusses lived experience and its psychological implications. In a phenomenological analysis of an experience, we need to examine the subjective world of the actor and scrutinize how the subjective world is interpreted through experiences. Here, language is of great significance. We experience our experiences, and we put our experiences into language. Understanding and experience provide a level of understanding that is distinct from the level of knowledge. Understanding and experience are linked to the ontological psychology of the experience, whereas knowing about an experience occurs at an epistemological level. Knowing about choices is a far cry from understanding choices in the process of an action.

Choice-making is the exercise of control. To acknowledge control suggests the acknowledgment of having choices. If control is perceived to be dependent on a nonsustainable source, the phenomenological experience of control ultimately stands in contrast with the implication of control. Taking away control would impose detrimental and harmful consequences.

Langer's further studies on control provided a relationship between perceived control and the exploration of possibilities (2005, 2009). A phenomenological analysis of perceived control may underpin the process of Langer's further research on mindfulness and its implications for perceived control. Langer focused on mindfulness as the key to having choices. She defined mindfulness as "a flexible state of mind in which we are actively engaged in the present, noticing new things and sensitive to context" (2000, p. 220).

Again, there needs to be a distinction between two major perspectives on mindfulness. One is associated with Eastern philosophy and Buddhism, where meditation appears to be the main tool of mindfulness. The work by Kabat-Zinn moves in line with this perspective (see Kabat-Zinn, 1994).

The other version of mindfulness, known as Langerian mindfulness, is associated with an experimental psychological approach with a continuous focus on creating and restructuring mindsets and perspectives along with flexibility, openness, and a proactive phenomenological presence in the moment.

Discussing the distinction between these two versions of mindfulness, Crum and Lyddy (2014) indicated that "Eastern mindfulness shines a clear light of unbiased and unattached awareness on existing mindsets whereas Langerian mindfulness involves a continual process or restructuring and creating mindsets anew" (p. 954).

Films can be discussed in terms of their power to demonstrate control, lack of control, agency, lack of agency, and their implications. Movies such

Films and Emotion 65

Dead Poets Society (1989).

Dead Poets Society (1989).

as *Dead Poets Society* (1989), *October Sky* (1999), *Gran Torino* (2008), *Forrest Gump* (1994), and *Super Size Me* (2004) are examples of movies that demonstrate control or lack of control.

In discussing the content of emotional regulation, emotional management, and agency with clients, clinicians can suggest movies that elucidate the consequences of self-regulation or lack of emotional management, agency, or a choice-oriented approach in life.

Heat of the Night (1967) portrays the story of a black man who is subjected to discrimination, aspersion, oppression, racism, and prejudice merely because he is Black. Notwithstanding all types of pressures and turmoil, the man composes himself with equanimity and tranquility,

66 *Films and Emotion*

calmness, and peace, and presents himself with patience, perseverance, agency, leadership, emotional intelligence, self-awareness, and values.

The questions for clients would be:

1   What is it in this man who can behave so calmly in the midst of hardships?
2   Where does he get the virtues of composure and calmness from?
3   Can this be modeled?
4   How does he choose to remain calm?
5   How can one explain his agency?
6   What else could have occurred if he had reacted impulsively?

Therapeutic discussions of emotions in the context of films may include emotional awareness, emotional management, understanding emotions in others, and emotional expressiveness.

Clients can be encouraged to watch a film and detect examples of emotional expressiveness. For instance, clients can be invited to watch *Scarlet Street* (1945) and find how contradictory emotions intermingle with one another and bring about emotional abduction.

Scarlet Street (1945) is a classic movie about a man (Chris) with an almost ordinary job who is not happy with his marriage and bumps into an attractive woman. The woman is aligned with a con artist, and they both set out to deceive the man through concocted ploys and games.

The film offers a rich repertoire of emotional taxonomy in various stages and demonstrates how emotional plays can overshadow the right decision making. Deeply smitten and with the turmoil at home and the external unrest, the man, who is also a painter, is manipulated into a dark and destructive path of annihilation.

The movie illustrates the tyranny of emotional influence and its effects on decision making. The man is seduced into believing that the woman loves him. Infatuated by the seductive power of love that quenches his emotional thirst, the man is shocked to learn that his world of dreams has nothing but mirages of illusion.

The movie can help the audience to ponder and reflect on the following questions:

1   How does Chris succumb to emotional abduction where emotions control him?
2   What else could he have done under these circumstances?
3   The woman (Kitty) and her con artist boyfriend (Johnny) manipulate Chris to steal money from both his wife and his company. Is Chris responsible for that?
4   What would Chris have done if his wife had demonstrated a caring and supportive role in his life? Could Chris have said no to Kitty's requests?

Films and Emotion 67

5　What would you have done if you had been in Chris's shoes?
6　How do you see the role of emotional expressiveness in the story? Passive, aggressive, or assertive?

In addition to the previously mentioned items, the session in therapy may focus on discussing the role of emotions in life and their modes of expressiveness. The client can be invited to sit back and examine how his or her life may have been shrouded through emotional muddiness on different occasions and how those occasions may have clouded his or her power of agency.

A movie may depict a kaleidoscopic array of emotions. Anger, sadness, surprise, hatred, happiness, joy, shame, and guilt are some of the very fundamental emotions that may be illustrated in movies.

Inviting clients to realize the experience of emotions about emotions may be of great importance here. The meta experiences of emotions may be discussed and examined in the context of the analytical focus on the emotional configuration presented in specific movies.

Scarlet Street (1945) is exemplified in the list of movies that present meta experiences of emotions. A man who is used to doing his work in a routinized manner suddenly has an emotional experience where he finds himself fraught with love and affection. Soon he finds out that he has been masterfully deceived and beguiled. A different and antagonizing emotion follows right after the first emotion. He gets confused once he perceives his emotions as problematic, and he undertakes avoidance strategies to deal with his confusing emotional experience.

In *A Christmas Carol* (1951), a movie that portrays a wide spectrum of emotions, one may see the change of emotions as the attitudes undergo transformations. Notice the following quote from Ebenezer Scrooge:

> How shall I ever understand this world? There is nothing on which it is so hard as poverty, and yet, there is nothing it condemns with such severity as the pursuit of wealth.

Now, notice the following from the Ghost of Jacob Marley:

> Hello, Ebenezer. I've been waiting here for you; I heard you were coming down today. I thought I'd be here to greet you; show you to your new office ... no one else wanted to.

> See the phantoms filling the sky around you. They astound you. I can tell, these inhabitants of hell. Poor wretches whom the hand of heaven ignores. Beware, beware, beware, lest their dreadful fate be yours!

An examination of emotional tones in the abovementioned sentences and their implications may open spaces for acknowledging the importance of

68 *Films and Emotion*

emotional expressiveness, which may be implicitly embedded within the parlance of speakers.

Emotions may be explicitly or implicitly depicted in movies. The following from *Beauty and the Beast* (1991) may reveal simple layers of emotions and emotional expressiveness:

BELLE: I want much more than this provincial life.
BELLE: I want adventure in the great, wide somewhere.

Therapists may discuss the following questions and examine their implications with their clients as they watch specific films:

1 What types of emotions do you observe in the given film in general?
2 Do you see any attempt toward emotional regulation and emotional management in the film?
3 Are there any instances in the film where one may notice the meta experiences of emotions?
4 Are there any demonstrations of primary and secondary emotions in the film? Primary emotions are the basic and fundamental emotional responses to an event or a situation. Secondary emotions constitute the emotional responses to the primary emotions. *A Place in the Sun* (1951), a classic movie, and *Unsane* (2018), *Hacksaw Ridge* (2016), and *Ali's Wedding* (2017), contemporary movies, portray different levels of primary and secondary emotions.
5 Do you see any examples of emotional expressiveness in the movie where one comfortably expresses one's emotions?
6 What are the applications of emotional awareness in one's life?
7 What are some of the positive emotions that may be found in the given films?
8 What are some of the negative emotions that may be found in the given films?
9 How do you see the emotional expressiveness in both words and actions in the given films?
10 Are there examples of primary and secondary emotions in the film? For instance, being sad after being angry?
11 Are there examples in the film where you may see the passive expressiveness versus aggressive modes of expressiveness or assertiveness versus aggressiveness?
12 Are there examples indicating the intensity of emotions in the film?
13 Are there examples where the characters are overcome by emotions?
14 Are there examples of emotional management right after emotional awareness in the given films?

9 Films and Global Wisdom

Attempts to enhance clients' well-being and wisdom lie at the center of a therapeutic goal. Understanding the underlying elements of well-being helps both clients and therapists to adopt an appropriate and working agenda to facilitate the process of well-being.

There are perspectives that emphasize the idiographic approach, emphasizing the individual being unique in his or her own context. This perspective traces its roots to philosophers such as Kierkegaard, who believed in the individuality of the person and his unique and distinct existential and ontological being, thus disapproving any nomothetic view where the commonality of human beings is underlined and delineated.

From an idiographic point of view (see Bruner, 1986, 1990; Gergen, 1991; Kvale, 1992; Shotter & Gergen, 1989), there may hardly be possible to discuss common core potentials among human beings.

On the other hand, there are movies like *The Karate Kid* (2010), *Tuesdays With Morrie* (1999), *Les Misérable* (1998), and *Nafas* (2016) that entail a message for people all around the globe regardless of age, culture, and language.

These movies also demonstrate and represent a great sense of wisdom shared by both Eastern and Western perspectives (see Sternberg, 1990, 1998).

Wisdom-oriented movies are ones that bring about sagacity and perspicacity, insight, and understanding beyond formal intelligence. They help one cry and laugh along with the tintinnabulation of the universal messages of what makes human beings human in terms of values, nature, togetherness, and meaning.

The act of watching films itself may give rise to an intentionality to be open toward experience. This openness would facilitate the process of reflecting on significant questions of life and living. Movies may help us understand how we may be stranded in our mindsets, and we may not pay attention to alternative ways of looking at things. Hitchcock's movie *Breakdown* (1955) depicts the story of two different states: one in power and one in full desperation and weakness. The shift from the state of power to the state of weakness and inability is so quick. It is a cogent demonstration of how the mundane humdrum of our life may cloud the nature of our genuine awareness.

DOI: 10.4324/9780429441431-9

Titanic (1997).

Sternberg's (1990, 1998) theory of wisdom focuses on balance in intrapersonal, interpersonal, and extrapersonal domains of interests. According to Sternberg, wisdom looks for common good. This sense of wisdom may be well delineated through films that focus on the common good. Movies can create values and bring our attention to the collective wisdom of our ages and its implications for our world today. This understanding of wisdom may help us understand how human beings may be connected to one another where vital questions of life and living are concerned. Extracting common good, common interests, common sufferings, common concerns, and common interests are displayed in movies.

Titanic (1997), *The Adventures of Robinhood* (1938), *The Godfather* (1972), *A Space Odyssey* (1968), *and Back to the Future* (1990) may all entail themes including love, justice, happiness, and family and humanity. Movies are thus powerful resources to awaken an interest in listening to universal themes.

Celebrating the possibility of looking at multiple perspectives and displaying a high degree of tolerance when confronting ambiguities are potentially embedded in many movies: movies may bring light into the easily forgotten realities of life.

The following quote from the movie *The Pursuit of Happyness* (2006) may provide opportunities to discuss themes and concepts that can be of great avail for a discussion on the growth of wisdom.

CHRISTOPHER: Hey, dad, you wanna hear something funny? There was a man who was drowning, and a boat came, and the man on the boat said, "Do you need help?" and the man said, "God will save me." Then another boat came, and he tried to help him, but he said, "God will save me," then he drowned and went to Heaven. Then the man told God, "God, why didn't you save me?" and God said, "I sent you two boats, you dummy!"

Films and Global Wisdom   71

The movie illustrates the power of perspective in giving rise to choices. Empowerment, choices, and possibilities are sequentially displayed in a potpourri of interactions.

Despite the fact that movies may bring about provocative and thoughtful moments where wisdom can be explored, discussed, and delineated, movies purport that wisdom is not abundantly available among people. The movies *The Karate Kid* (2010) and *Tuesdays With Morrie* (1999) substantiate the scarcity of wisdom and its invaluable presence if it is ever found. Sagacity and depth, perspicacity, and illuminating insight are not very often found in people, and the aforementioned movies underline its rarity.

On the other hand, movies may serve as evocative tools to help us delve into questions that may lead to wisdom development. When watching a movie where genocide is depicted or racism is displayed, the follow-up questions can concentrate on the costs of such tragedies, the impact of such catastrophes on people's lives, their annihilation, and their destruction.

I Am a Fugitive From a Chain Gang (1939) is a classic movie that pictures human atrocities and injustice. A man is sentenced to 10 years of imprisonment for a crime that he has not committed. The crime is robbing a diner, held at gunpoint by a villain.

Notice the following quotes from different parts of *I Am a Fugitive From a Chain Gang* (1939) to see the tenor of the parlance:

JAMES ALLEN: Do you mind if we stay here awhile, or must you go home?
HELEN: There are no musts in my life. I'm free, white, and twenty-one.
PETE: I'm hungry. What would you say to a hamburger?
JAMES ALLEN: What would I say to a hamburger? Boy. I'd take Mr. Hamburger by the hand and say, "Pal, I haven't seen you for a long, long time."
HELEN: How do you live?
JAMES ALLEN: I steal.

The follow-up questions may focus on how human beings have been subjugated to injustice and oppression by the name of justice. How have people been silently subjected to exploitation, deception, and maltreatment? What is it that can be done to prevent such destructive moves against humanity?

The point is to use the given movies to bring about a broader awareness of vital issues that can have universal implications. The awareness can be applied to self-awareness. Movies can lead the discussion of gaining self-knowledge and a profound insight into oneself. Understanding and being in touch with one's feelings, competencies, emotions, and goals would unfold their importance as one reflects on the relationship between what the movie portrays and what one can ponder. This does not suggest that

72 Films and Global Wisdom

one is copying the movie and a mimicry occurs between the viewer and what is seen. On the contrary, the movie can highlight prompts that may underscore the significance of looking into one's internal world.

For instance, the movie *Dial M for Murder* (1954) may be discussed in terms of emotional regulation, emotional understanding, and the possibility of looking at oneself as both an observer and an actor.

The goal here is to awaken a potentially vibrant resource in human beings to reflect on the event, the consequences of the event, the process of happenings, and, more important, the likelihood of getting connected to the event beyond the geographical, ethnic, racial, and cultural boundaries.

The Berlin wisdom paradigm and Max Planck's studies of wisdom focus on wisdom. Wisdom is characterized by expert knowledge in the meaning and conduct of life and in the fundamental pragmatics of life (i.e., life planning, life management, and life review). Five criteria are discussed here to assess wisdom-related knowledge: rich factual knowledge, rich procedural knowledge, life span contextualism, value relativism, and uncertainty (see, for instance, Baltes et al., 2002; Baltes & Smith, 1990; Baltes & Staudinger, 2000; Dittmann-Kohli & Baltes, 1990). Wisdom, in this paradigm, addresses existential issues in life and discusses questions concerning the meaning of life.

It is interesting to note that Max Planck's studies on wisdom reiterate that imagination and experiencing an imaginary conversation may enhance a sense of wisdom (see, for example, Baltes et al. 2002).

In this regard, movies may be discussed to underscore the importance of looking at an action from the outside and exploring it from the inside. The dialectics of becoming both an observer and actor may move in line with an in-depth connection to the phenomenological experience. Therapists can encourage clients to look at a given movie's episodes at either the macro or micro level and see how the episode(s) may open up lessons that can apply to personal life situations. If a client, for instance, has problems with anger management, the episode may provide lessons on emotional regulation and emotional management with an aim to look at the consequences of unbridled anger.

The point of discussing global wisdom here goes beyond this level: The intention is to see how specific movies may espouse connections that can apply to human beings in general. The focus is expanded here to include a general universal topic such as pain or suffering that can apply to human beings regardless of their belonging to one culture or one race.

The discernment of global wisdom and its implications may help clients understand how films may provide a platform for thinking beyond the boxes, beyond stereotypes, and even beyond what the media has programmed people.

Films and Global Wisdom 73

In *Les Misérables* (1998), for instance, the connection is extended to reach human delicacies and human perceptiveness beyond the mundane strata of daily engagements.

The following quotes from *Les Misérables* (1998) may bring moments of cogitation, contemplation, reflexivity, and reflection to scrutinize the cynosure of life, living, and meaning at metacognitive and meta experience levels. *Metacognition* here refers to thinking about thinking, and *meta experience* refers to a secondary emotional experience about a primarily emotional experience.

MARIUS: If we can't win today, then none of us have a future.
VALJEAN: You have love. That's the only future God gives us.
BISHOP: Don't ever forget, you've promised to become a new man.
VALJEAN: Promise? Why are you doing this?
BISHOP: Jean Valjean, my brother, you no longer belong to evil. With this silver, I have bought your soul. I've ransomed you from fear and hatred, and now I give you back to God.

Therapists can discuss these movies with clients to give them a sense of meaning and direction.

The following questions may be used to provide clients with an in-depth understanding of the role of wisdom in movies:

1 What types of messages do you see in the film that may resonate with everyone in the world?
2 How do you feel about these messages?
3 What makes people cry together or laugh together based on the given scene of the film?
4 What are the implications of such messages for the whole world?
5 Based on the specific scene of the film, how do you distinguish knowledge from wisdom?
6 How do you see the relationship between proactive behavior a great sense of wisdom?
7 What are the strategies to enhance wisdom in personal life and interpersonal life?
8 How do the given movies open up the space for discussing a higher tolerance for ambiguity?
9 How do the given movies under discussion bring about a perspective that is not bound by existing rules?
10 How do the given movies open up space for reflecting on the existential meaning of life?
11 How do the selected movies bring about the importance of reflecting on leading a meaningful life?
12 How do the selected movies discuss how to deal with challenges and problems in one's personal life?

74 *Films and Global Wisdom*

13 How do the selected movies bring about a change in one's perspective toward a lie's fundamental issues, including the mortality of the material world?

14 How do the given movies give rise to an elaborate discussion on ways to care for others in general?

10 Films, Signs, and Symbols

Films may be taken as a text and are thus analyzable from different perspectives. One way of looking at films may begin with an exploration of the constellation of signs and their meanings and implications. A *sign* entails the combination of a signifier and a signified. The *signifier* is the sound image that transports the signified, and the *signified* is a concept that refers to something. A sign reveals the correlation between the signified and signifier (de Saussure, 1966). A sign is not the signifier. What the sign refers to is the *referent*.

According to Italian semiotician Umberto Eco (1976), there are often cases and examples where the referent of a sign is not a real object or a subject but the signified or signifier of another sign. Thus, the signified or the signifier of a sign correlation can, in turn, be either the signifier or the signified of another sign correlation. It is in the juxtaposition of signs that signification occurs.

Films present a plethora of signs and symbols, and they may reveal an interconnected and interrelated complex of other existing signs and symbols.

One may look at a film and decode and dig into the apparent signs that manifest themselves in the first perceptible level. For instance, when watching a movie such as *The Shawshank Redemption* (1994), the easily accessible presentation of signs may highlight the story of prisoners, their suffering, their maltreatment by the wardens, etc. The film, however, may depict other systems of signification within the film to the effect that one can discover and discern other potentiated available resources of sensibility within the system of signs.

For example, one may fathom the relationship between hope and personhood, perseverance and emancipation in action, and responses that appear to operate in different levels of Tim Robbin's performance.

The following quote may be exemplified as a complex set of signs that embody different levels of significations.

ANDY DUFRESNE: Remember, Red, hope is a good thing, maybe the best of things. And no good thing ever dies.

DOI: 10.4324/9780429441431-10

76 *Films, Signs, and Symbols*

The sentences are here indicative of different potential significations. On one level, one may notice the importance of hope in the statement and its implications. On another level, one may discuss the impact of hope in its manifestation as the best of things, a panacea in life. On another level, one may reflect on hope as an eternally influencing element with an inextinguishable power. These levels of analyses may occur in different conceptual systems, which may produce sundry demonstrations of practical positions.

In other words, one may place the statement in a secular system of thoughts and merely focus on the role and functions of hope. This might entail even a biological analysis where hope gives rise to a high level of serotonin and dopamine and a reduction in cortisol.

In the meantime, one may put the discussion in a theologically oriented system of thinking and may discuss the relationship between hope and a belief in God, where despair is considered as turning your back on God.

These levels of analyses may not simply pop up in the first encounter with the statement and may need an in-depth exploration of the relationship among the existing systems of signs. The important point to consider here is a rigorous understanding of the underlying structures of interpretive means and their referential perspectives.

To put it differently, the systems of analysis within the selected repertories of signs may occur in accordance with the pre-postulated epistemic systems of inquiry.

Suppose the epistemic system, for instance, concentrates on the perceptible existential levels and their objective and tangible sensibility. In that case, one may draw on findings that may differ from another system where the invisible levels of existence are taken into consideration.

The film itself may open up this space as one may easily notice in movies such as *The Portrait of Jennie* (1948) or *Contact* (1997). The film presents a recognizable system of signification where the existential system goes beyond the ephemeral layers of the unknown. In other instances, one may relate the theme and the content to the alternative modes of signification where the level of analysis points to an ontologically sensible configuration beyond the material world.

In the movies *Away From Her* (2006) and *Iris* (2001), one may begin to ponder the transcendental sense of meaning-making beyond the story's obvious levels.

It may thus be safe to say that films may be examined in terms of signs and symbols in two different material and immaterial systems.

Empirically speaking, there are numerous research findings that discuss and present the two different systems together (Goleman, 2003; Lipton, 2005; Pert, 1997).

The distinctions mentioned above and understanding may lead us toward a more strenuous examination of films, signs, and symbols in broader contexts.

At first glance, one may tend to use signs and symbols interchangeably, which may be fine if taken superficially. Nonetheless, one may need to be

Films, Signs, and Symbols 77

aware of the subtle differences for the sake of our previously mentioned discussion on two varying operating systems of analysis in the perceptible and immaterial domains of sensibility.

One system that is mainly characterized in the Western mainstream epistemological and ontological understanding of signification concentrates on signs and their implications in the word's materialistic sense.

The emphasis is then on the conceptual and practical roles of signs in espousing the essence of meaning-making, sensibility, and plausibility.

The first serious work on the sovereignty of the signs was presented by the Swiss semiologist Ferdinand de Saussure (1857–1913). Then, Charles Sanders Peirce (1839–1914) explicated the realm of signs and discussed their three different systems: icons, indexes, and symbols, with their respective focus on resemblance, cause and effect, and convention.

Italian semiotician Umberto Eco (1976) brought a more elaborate presentation on the range of signs and discussed that there are often cases and examples where the referent of a sign is not a real object or a subject but the signified or signifier of another sign. Therefore, the signified or the signifier of a sign correlation can, in turn, be either the signifier or the signified of another sign correlation.

Signification emerges in the dialogical relationship of signs and the connections between the signifier and signified. The intellectual enlightenment and its outcry for rationality, positivism, control, prediction, and certitude were influential factors that helped establish signs and their discursive manifestations.

The intellectual enlightenment defined rationality with a focus on the world of the visible and prescribed modes of knowing. The prescription verified the templates of sensibility within the borders and constituents of the visible. Logical positivism, empiricism, and their expansionist clamor grew in the midst of such parades. The study of signs was thus inspired by an emphatic pattern of rationality and its explicit prescriptive implications.

Neither the semiotics nor the semiology of signs was given a chance to leap beyond the prescribed forms of rationality and sensibility. Therefore, they constructed their rational-oriented approaches and celebrated their certitude of signs without deconstructing their own underlying ontological and epistemological constituents. Along with the overarching power of the signs, "I" descended to be identical to "body" and "body" served as the main source of the interpretive inquiry. The idolization of the body and its tyrannical multiplicities ushered in the hollowness of "I" and the alienation of the self.

Explicating the sovereignty of a material-oriented world of signs, Johnston (2001), wrote,

> From Marilyn Monroe to the Spice Girls, from Arnold Schwarzenegger to O. J. Simpson, from William Taft to Bill Clinton, to your own naked form reflected in the mirror each morning, we are taught to read bodies as symbols displaying and revealing hidden "truths"

78 *Films, Signs, and Symbols*

about the individual and his or her behaviors. Any discussion of the body becomes complex and muddled as one tries to analyze how and why certain body types are attributed to certain meanings.

(p. xvii)

Films can be analyzed and discussed in terms of their embodiments in the materially evocative domain of signification. The movies *Showgirls* (1995) and *Striptease* (1996) portray how the mentality of the signification above may operate at different levels of presentation. This does not suggest that one may not look for other levels of signification in such movies, but the point is to elaborate how the movies, as mentioned earlier, may tend to prime a focus on the systems of signs within the material epistemic signification.

Historically speaking, the despotism of signs contained and limited the definition of intelligibility and circumscribed the approaches to knowing. The subscription to sign-oriented patterns and paradigms became the criteria for sensibility, competence, and superiority. The tyranny of signs in the context as mentioned above has been challenged for years.

Critiquing the authoritative presence of such sensibility, Shotter (1993) indicated that

in fulfilling our responsibilities as competent and professional academics, we must write systematic texts; we run the risk of being accounted incompetent if we do not. Until recently, we have taken such texts for granted as a neutral means to use how we please. This, I now want to claim, is a mistake, and now we must study their influence.

(p. 25)

The government of signs promoted exclusive interpretation for thinking, learning, and education and thus elbowed aside numerous other possible forms of understanding. The executive powers of such exclusion gave rise to a discourse of power where sensibility had to be ratified by specific channels. The cultivation and socialization of the most available perspective on signs generated numerous forms of reliance on the established modes of knowing.

Filmmaking was embedded within the discourse of rationality and sensibility as prescribed by the intellectual enlightenment and a utilitarian propensity. This, in turn, highlighted the establishment of a language and a generative metalanguage where the paradigmatic and syntagmatic analysis and assessment of approaches and practices borrowed their sensibility from the binding source of intellectuality based on the rational understanding of signs. The imperial power of signs and their inducing command of rationality turned out to be inexorably linked to the community of both educators and learners in a broader context. Michal Oakeshott had a notion of such implications when he wrote that:

Flattered by circumstance and linked with ancient heresy, an attempt was made to promote "science" as itself a "culture" in which human

Films, Signs, and Symbols 79

beings identified themselves in relation to "things" and their "empire over things," but it now deceives nobody; boys do not elect for the "science sixth" expecting to achieve self-knowledge, but for vocational reasons.

(As cited in Barrow & Woods, 2006, p. 35)

The idolization of signs and their emphasis on linear thinking also generated a utilitarian objective within the field of film making focused on packaging everything within the so-called standardization of learning and teaching; it changed education into a business plan where the agenda was to sell the right form of thinking and the proper way of learning. Development, improvement, growth, and thinking were strongly assessed based on their adaptability to signs' ontology. An obsession with techniques was highly consecrated.

Thus, as actualized in conventional practices and institutions, education enacted the criteria of sense-making by virtue of its own signs. Education indoctrinated, blocking alternatives of seeing, perceiving, and knowing, monopolizing its own as the first and the foremost reflection of reality as submitted in its own sign(s). It is in line with the hazards of such obsessions that Habermas (1973) discussed modern society's failure to distinguish between the practical and technical.

The real difficulty in the relation of theory to praxis does not arise from this new function of science as a technological force but rather because we are no longer able to distinguish between practical and technical power. Yet even a civilization that has been rendered scientific is not granted dispensation from practical questions. Therefore, a particular danger arises when the process of scientification transgresses the limit of reflection of rationality confined to the technological horizon. For then no attempt at all is made to attain a rational consensus on citizens concerned with the practical control of their destiny. Its place is taken by the attempt to attain technical control over history by perfecting society's administration, an attempt that is just as impractical as it is unhistorical.

Questioning our taken-for-granted assumptions in the realm of signs, Herda (1999) indicated that "most typically, we take for granted our social actions, structured or patterned by language, and we fail to see them" (p. 24). She revisited our thinking and called for deconstructing the assumptions governed by the system of signs.

Herda (1999) noted that the lack of depth of the current usage of the term "thinking" in the critical thinking bandwagon undermines adult or young leaders' potential to reflect, learn, and act in meaningful ways. Looking for a critical curriculum development that can observe its own imposition of assumptions, Snyder (2002) put the courage into words:

we need to develop pedagogical and curriculum frameworks that seek to endow students with a sense of their place in the new global system, but also with the capacity to view that system critically. At the very least, we can help our students to engage in local forms of cultural critique.

(p. 181)

80   *Films, Signs, and Symbols*

In discussing the sovereignty of signs and its implications for films as described above, we may want to look at an alternative perspective by Carl Jung (1875–1961), who departed from the sign-stricken domain and highlighted the significance of symbols along the path of signs.

Jung indicated that our life and, above all, our health is in dire need of symbols. He indicated that a life where symbols are concealed into oblivion generates neurosis, alienation, parochialism, estrangement, superficiality, and entanglement.

He began discussing the significance of symbols by comparing them with the signs where signs constantly focus on the known, on the obvious, on the rational, on the visible, on the accessible, and on the available, whereas symbols concentrate on the unknown, the mysterious, the ambiguous, and the unconscious.

On such preliminary discussions, Jung suggested,

> A word or an image is symbolic when it implies something more than its obvious and immediate meaning. It has a wider unconscious aspect that is never precisely defined or fully explained. Nor can anyone hope to define or explain it. As the mind explores the symbol, it is led to ideas that lie beyond the grasp of reason.
>
> (Jung et al., 1964, pp. 20–21)

Jung questioned the containment of reality within the prescriptive modes of signs and argued that reality is not to be bound by the visible; the sphere of existence cannot be limited to the domain of the visible signs and the rationality that seeks the sensibility within the visible world would be inadequate to reflect and represent the magnitude of reality.

Existence, according to Jung, can be explored and understood within the domain of signs but cannot be restricted and contained within signs. The layers of existence are far too extensive to be circumscribed within the territorial integrity of signs. Jung went beyond the limitations of the reading of our perceived reality through signs and highlighted the significance of understanding a new and yet independent realm of existence, meaning-making, and sensibility; that is, the realm of symbols.

Illustrating the unreality of our reality, Tacey (2007) wrote,

> Our minds are conditioned to think that only what we can see and touch is real, but Jung questioned this view, and his psychology is a challenge to our understanding of reality. Jung was an unsettling thinker because he introduced the notion that the evidence of our sense is illusory and that common sense is nothing more than a construct of external conditioning.
>
> (p. 12)

Films, Signs, and Symbols 81

Revolutionizing the modes of thinking, Jung challenged the absolutism of the scientific discourse and their monarchical manifestations in endorsing the validity of the truth through logical positivism and linear forms of thinking. He yearned for a genuine search for knowledge and wisdom and opened the possibility of exploring the genius of inspiration and intuition as real modes of knowing and learning.

> We have become rich in knowledge but poor in wisdom. Our interest center of gravity has switched over to the materialistic side, whereas the ancients preferred a mode of thought nearer to the fantastic type. To the classical mind, everything was still saturated with mythology.
> (As cited in Tacey, 2007, p. 15)

On Jung's vital message, Tacey (2007) wrote:

> We tend to think of myths and religions as "untrue" and of dreams as "distortions" of reality. But for Jung, they are expressions of a truth that is truer than literal truth. This is Jung's vital message, linking him to the "perennial philosophy" and wisdom traditions that originate from Heraclitus, Socrates, and Plato. Socrates said truth is not self-evident, and Jung would agree. What we see, and what we seem, is not the whole truth. Our knowledge is not reliable; it is partial and undermined by the fact that the unconscious has a separate truth dimension, of which we are mostly oblivious. Ironically, deeper truth resides in what we habitually dismiss as an illusion, fantasy, myth, and distortion. This may be one reason why, in an age governed by science and logic, our entertainment is saturated with fantasy, mythic stories, and legends: a compensatory process has risen in popular culture. The reason we have lost access to the deeper truth, for Jung, is that we have lost access to the symbolic language that discloses it. Our world blinded consciousness has made a successful adaptation to external reality, but the cost has been an atrophy of our symbolic life.
> (p. 15)

A Jungian understanding of films leaps beyond the monosomy and univocity and searches for multiplicities of meaning while celebrating multiple ways of knowing. This understanding can be embedded in alternative ways of looking into the hermeneutics of films and their contextual cognitive, emotional, and behavioral components.

For this, Jung's project of symbols complies with Ricoeur's (1991) understanding of language where inventiveness, novelty, creativity, and innovation unfold their creational power through a language that goes beyond the sign and sign-oriented limitations.

A Jungian understanding of symbols helps us understand the power of intuition and inspiration in enriching the modes of expressiveness; it is

82 *Films, Signs, and Symbols*

through these powers that creativity unfolds itself. Jung (1971) pinpointed the significance of such powers:

> Every creative individual whatsoever owes all that is greatest in his life to fantasy. The dynamic principle of fantasy is play, a characteristic also of the child, and as such, it appears inconsistent with the principle of serious work. But without this playing with fantasy, no creative work has ever come to birth. The debt we owe to the play of imagination is incalculable.
>
> (p. 63)

Bruner (1986) presented the narrative metaphor in sociology and focused on the interpretation of a text in its broadest sense; culture, itself, was considered a text with multifarious layers of meaning. On the relationship between experience, narrative, and meaning, Bruner (1991) indicated that "we organize our experience and our memory of human happening mainly in the form of narrative stories, excuses, myths, reasons for doing and not doing, and so on" (p. 4).

Jungian presentation of symbols protests the overarching idolization of science in its linear and empirical exclusive version. It vociferously challenges the unquestionably established paradigms that foster nothing but the transformation of learners into control and conditioning objects. As Jung stated, any approach "that satisfies the intellect alone can never be practical, for the totality of the psyche can never be grasped by the intellect alone" (1953, p. 76). He explained,

> It cannot be the aim of education to turn out rationalists, materialists, specialists, technicians, and others of the kind who, unconscious of their origins, are precipitated abruptly into the present and contribute to the disorientation and fragmentation of society.
>
> (As cited in Frey-Rohn et al., 1974, p. 182)

A challenge against the subjugation of signs and its reductionism can be tracked down in and among the voices that break the reliance on signs' enchainment. Bellah et al. (1991), for instance, referred to a wide gap

> between technical reason, the knowledge with which we design computers or analyze the structure of DNA, and practical or moral reason, the ways we understand how we should live ... What we need to know is not simply how to build a powerful computer or how to redesign DNA but precisely and above all, how to do with that knowledge.
>
> (p. 44)

A Jungian understanding of symbols would facilitate looking at films with more depth and vigilance; it would help us openly examine and explore the taken-for-granted assumptions and critically look at the construction

Films, Signs, and Symbols 83

of knowledge. This understanding becomes sensitive to how language creates constructs, transforms, and positions.

Ha'iri Yazdi (1992) questioned the ubiquitous implications of signs and challenged the entrenchment of the sign-oriented interpretation of knowing and its concentrated mobilization for searching the sensibility within the fences of linear forms of thinking and logical positivism. He highlighted the sensibility of mysticism as a way of understanding while substantiating and corroborating a wide spectrum of knowing.

Ha'iri (1992) revolted against modern Western philosophy's exclusion of "claims of awareness from the domain of human knowledge" and substantiated that the meaningfulness of the Modern ways of knowing brand "mere expressions of fervor or as leaps of imagination" (p. 5).

When knowing is not just a gerund in the air, when knowing turns out to be, in the words of Ha'iri Yazdi (1992), "being," and language becomes an "action" in the words of Habermas (1979), we may better understand the ontological aspect of signs in terms of their creation. With a focus on knowing as being, Ha'iri Yazdi (1992) indicated,

> The inquiry into the nature of the relationship between knowledge and word knowing does not mean anything other than being. In this ontological state of human consciousness, the subject-object relationship's constitutive dualism is overcome and submerged into a unitary simplex of the reality of the self that is nothing other than self-object knowledge. From this unitary simplex, the nature of self-object consciousness can, in turn, be derived.
>
> (p. 1)

According to Jung, with the expansion of signs and dissipation of symbols, the fragmentation and disorientation grew with the ever-increasing emergence of self-alienation. The disappearance of symbols from human life took away the wholeness, and thus the fragmentation was associated with illness. Jung stated,

> It seems that side by side with the decline of religious life, the neuroses grow noticeably more frequent. We are living undeniably in a period of greatest restlessness, nervous tension, confusion, and disorientation of outlook.
>
> (As cited in Tacey, 2007, p. 97)

On the spiritual dimension of healing and its connectedness to understanding the role of symbols, Jung said,

> During the past thirty years, people from all the civilized countries of the earth have consulted me. Many hundreds of patients have passed through my hands, the greater number being Protestants, a lesser number of Jews, and not more than five or six believing Catholics.

84 *Films, Signs, and Symbols*

Among all my patients in the second half of life—that is to say, over thirty-five—there has not been one whose problem in the last resort was not finding a religious outlook on life. It is safe to say that every one of them fell ill because he had lost what the living religions of every age have given to their followers, and none of them has been healed who did not regain his religious outlook. This, of course, has nothing to do with a particular creed or membership of a church.

(As cited in Tacey, 2007, pp. 85–86)

According to Jung, a perspective without attention to the role and the implications of symbols would lead to reductionism, parochialism, and consumerism. An understanding of the Jungian discourse of symbols would enhance the power of creativity and the gift of reflexivity. The Jungian discourse of symbols would invite both the learner and the teacher to go beyond the mastery of signs and celebrate the mystery of symbols; it is a promising preamble to vivify the enthusiasm of searching for multiple ways of knowing and understanding. How can educators promote thinking if they are already enmeshed in limiting packages of signification? How can learners explore new horizons of thinking if they are extensively and frequently exposed to the availability and accessibility of the sign-promoting discourses? How can the educational practices offer any depth if their layers of constitution are heavily ensconced in linear forms of engagement and positivist-oriented approaches? And how might learners learn to mindfully reconsider the correlation of the signifier and signified within the induced signification? If film viewers are consistently influenced by the socially and politically imposed signified, can they search for the analysis of correlation between signifier and signified without being mindfully active?

On the description of some of these engagements, Lasn (1999) wrote,

Advertisements are the most prevalent and toxic of mental pollutants. From the moment your radio alarm sounds in the morning to the wee hours of late-night TV, micro-jolts of commercial pollution flood into your brain at the rate of about three thousand marketing messages per day. Every day, an estimated 12 billion display ads, 3 million radio commercials, and more than 200,000 TV commercials are dumped into North America's collective unconscious.

(pp. 18–19)

How can film viewers reflect on their positions and reexamine their connectedness, socially, culturally, and politically, if they are bound to think through the sign-inducing forms and orders?

A Jungian understanding of symbols brings awareness of the privatization of individuals, their placement in a universe of simulacra, and their entrapment in the flamboyant spectacles that present themselves by the name of science. Just as signs lead us to ordinary transactions, recognition

Films, Signs, and Symbols 85

and understanding of symbols would provide profound reflexivity, deep contemplation, and sensitivity toward examining modes of being.

In the words of Tacey (2007), "The study of signs leads to semiotics, linguistics and discourse analysis. The study of symbols leads to mythology, religion and philosophy" (p. 11)

Jung's discourse of symbols illustrates the vitality of poetry and poetic understanding; it illuminates the merit of intuition, inspiration, and mythical understanding. Understanding Jung's symbols would explicate how a concentration on sign-driven programs and their focus on linear thinking may divest the viewers of voicing themselves and recognizing the value of their narratives, their "hills and valleys." It brings to life the inherent creativity that dwells within everyone, within each child.

Political and utilitarian policymaking seems to prefer and design sign-driven films where engagement in deep critical thinking and creative examination of the assumptions are not encouraged or are marginalized.

Warning against sign-inducing programs, Morgan (2002) argued,

> As students start to question "texts in the world," they also begin to question "texts in mind." They recognize that they are not necessarily the sole authors of "commonsense" beliefs but are instead subjects produced through language and discourse. From a post-structural perspective, such forms of understanding are necessary to imitate attention and action on social inequalities whose persistence is sustained by their seeming naturalness.
>
> (p. 156)

Jungian understanding of signs would offer the promise inherent when understanding. Interpretation is driven not by reading signs but by engaging in metonymic, mysterious, generative, and polysemic symbols.

To Ricoeur (1991a), "It is the task of poetry to make words mean as much as they can and not as little as they can" (p. 449). In and through poetry, one may say, language can be liberated from the constrictions of sign-driven discourse, and new layers of reality can be revealed.

Ricoeur (1991a) argued that "through this recovery of the capacity of language to create and re-create, we discover reality itself in the process of being created. So we are connected with this dimension of reality which is unfinished" (p. 462)

Speaking on the role of metaphor and the process of becoming for language, Ricoeur (1991a) described the language of poetry and its significant role: "language in the making celebrates reality in the making" (p. 462)

Making a distinction between the language of ordinary speech where the signs have established their authority and the language of poetry in dealing with reality, he remarkably presented a very striking characteristic of ordinary language versus the language of poetry:

86   *Films, Signs, and Symbols*

And the rest of our language in ordinary speech and so on has to do with reality as it is already done, as it is finished, as it is there in the sense of the closedness of what is, with its meaning which is already asserted by the consensus of wise people.

(Ricoeur, 1991b, p. 462)

Elaborating on the role of metaphor and its capacity for changing and shattering reality, Ricoeur (1991b) propounded that "with the metaphor, we experience the metamorphosis of both language and reality" (p. 85). He did not submit to the pervasive discourse of signs and its clamorous quest for defining the reality in sign-inducing exegesis. There is an attempt to reduce as much as possible this polysemy in scientific language, this plurivocity to univocity: one word–one sense. But "it is the task of poetry to make words mean as much as they can and not as little as they can. Therefore, not to elude or exclude this plurivocity but to cultivate it, make it meaningful, powerful, and bring back to language all its capacity of meaningfulness". (Ricoeur, 1991b, p. 449)

Eyes gazed and fixed at the flamboyant and bombastic discourse of signs, and its monolithic political glasses of validity may not be able to question the nakedness of the signs away from their disguising masks of admiration; the platitude is masquerading as the sine qua non of reality and the truth.

Ricoeur (1991b) identified the nudity of the emperor and the imperialism of the discourse of signs:

If it is true that poetry gives no information in terms of empirical knowledge, it may change our way of looking at things, a change which is no less real than empirical knowledge. What is changed by poetic language is our way of dwelling in the world. From poetry, we receive a new way of being in the world, of orienting ourselves in the world. Even if we say with Northrop Frye that poetic discourse gives articulation only to our moods, it is also true that moods and feelings have an ontological bearing. Through feelings, we find ourselves already located in the world. In this way, by articulating a mood, each poem projects a new way of dwelling. It opens up a new way of being for us.

(p. 85)

In *The Heart and Soul of Change: What Works in Therapy*, Hubble et al. (1999) brought together research that indicates that 85% of client change is due to nonspecific counseling or psychotherapeutic factors. They discussed issues such as spiritual faith and community members and their role as contributing 40% to client change, relationship factors 30%, and hope and expectancy 15%.

A symbol-oriented film analysis would appreciate art and literature's invaluable presence, whereas sign-oriented pedagogy would cunningly ignore them. In support for the presence of such symbol-promoting programs and their implications, Jung (1966a) indicated,

Films, Signs, and Symbols 87

The great secret of art and the creative process consists in the unconscious activation of an archetypal image and in elaborating and shaping this image into the finished work. By giving it shape, the artist translates it into the present language, making it possible for us to find the way back to the deepest springs of life.

(p. 82)

The mastery of signs produces a film analysis where techne replaces phronesis. The questions of ethics and values become superannuated except for the flirtations that can consume the leisure time of the significant players. The mastery of signs dehumanizes the individual and promotes consumerism, utilitarianism, intellectualism, absence, fragmentation, and reductionism.

The mystery of symbols would celebrate the power of inspiration, heart and spirit, imagination and intuition, mysticism and unconsciousness. Symbols link the earth to the sky and the mind to the heart. The mystery of symbols echoes the tintinnabulation of connectedness, wholeness, belonging, and togetherness; it calls for transcendence, moves toward above, and is brimming with awe. The hegemony of the sign and its underlying quest for power tends to sustain and reproduce voices that support the hegemonic predominance; voicing against the constituent rules of this hegemony would be considered one of the most supercilious acts; the subtle slavery of signs silences the questioning of the mastery of signs. A symbolic understanding of films would follow the avenues of mysticism, the meanders of wonder, the wild meadows of reflective imagination, and the dialectic of mindfulness and heartfulness. A symbolic understanding of films would promise an act of creativity. The act of creativity is not searching for sameness, is not in pursuit of congruence or compatibility, and is not moving toward convergence. Creativity is not bound to coherence, cohesiveness, conformity, correspondence, or consistency in a sign-oriented paradigm. Creativity may represent an act of revelation where things are revealed in light of creativity and unconsciousness, as it can be an act of disclosure where things are cryptically and yet creatively presented. Creativity is not dutifully at the service of the recognized order as it is not respectful of the relationships and their establishment within the government of signs. Creativity may bring chaos and disorder, but this chaotic situation is only a result of a comparison between the act of creativity and the previously identified system of order within the plane of signs.

Having taken into consideration the distinctions between signs and symbols in the aforementioned discussions in this chapter, therapists may want to encourage clients to observe and notice meanings and concepts that may not be visibly accessible. This does not suggest that therapists would impose their worldviews on their clients or manipulate them to embrace a spiritual or religious perspective.

Nonetheless, it opens up the way to broaden perspective during discussion when it comes to subjects of spirituality, religiousness, meaning in life, emptiness in life, values and goals, etc.

88 *Films, Signs, and Symbols*

This understanding helps the discussion focus on the metaphorical, mystical, and deeper layers of films such as *Cinderella* (2015), *The Wizard of Oz* (1939), and *Beauty and the Beast* (2017).

These three films may fall into an analysis within the sign-oriented perspective where the signifier and signified are embedded in the material paradigm. They can be exposed to a symbol-oriented analysis where the signification and the relationships between signifier and signified explore the possibility of an immaterial connection.

Therapists may bring attention to this symbolic propensity of films in their discussions with clients and ask them to examine the films' stories and their implications for universal themes and contents. Therapists may also help clients pay attention to religious coping strategies that unfold themselves in films.

The following questions may be taken into account when discussing films beyond the perceptible sign configuration:

1   Do you see any subject or theme in the films that may be universally applicable to other cultures in the world?
2   How do you see the role of a spiritual or religious belief in bringing meaning into life?
3   How do you see the film genre touch up questions of knowing beyond the material world?
4   Are there any coping strategies in the films that you think might be related to a religious or spiritual perspective?
5   Do you see any indication of an internal journey of self in the movie?
6   How do you see the movie approach the questions of existence? Does the movie validate any layers of existence beyond what we see and hear?
7   Are there themes in the film that may be universally connected to feelings and emotions beyond geography, race, language, and age?
8   The in-depth exploration of films as potential texts to demonstrate the epistemological and ontological perspectives provides the audience with affluent opportunities to experience metacognition and meta experiences of emotions and their philosophical and psychological implications.

11 Film Therapy in Action

Are there ways to enlighten the scope of therapy through the expansive use of films? How can therapists employ films in their discussions and practices? What new insights can be taken into consideration to enrich a broader understanding of films and their implementation? The following techniques and principles may elucidate the application and implications of films in therapeutic contexts:

1 **A film can be considered a text.** Clients need to receive an orientation that films may serve as very operable tools to develop awareness and direction. Movies can be recommended to illustrate the significance of an issue or demonstrate how others have dealt with similar problems or issues. Movies may also come into the discussion to indicate the dynamics of relationships, the effects of perspectives, the power of language, the importance of time and place, etc. Films may also be selected to provide empathy and understanding. Films can be decoded, analyzed, and interpreted. Clients can be encouraged to focus on the broader perspective of films as an expansive platform of communication that entails psychological themes. For instance, a film such as *To Kill a Mockingbird* (1962) can be selected for discussion and analysis. In the discussion and analysis, the atomic components may be aligned with a systematic format in that particular features of the film may be discussed and interpreted. The film's overall story, its plots, and its components may be exposed to a coherent analysis and interpretation. The previously mentioned discussions on the verbal, vocal, and visual arts of the film can be selected to broaden and strengthen the analysis.

2 **Films can be therapeutically effective.** Clients can be invited to watch a film and classify the genre, topics, scenes, relationships, categories, individuals, events, and techniques in the film based on the discussions and conversation in therapy sessions. The classification can be done in line with the presentation of the film and its contents, or it may be creatively constructed. For instance, the movie *Glengarry Glen Ross* (1992) may be analyzed through the social justice perspective or the

DOI: 10.4324/9780429441431-11

90 *Film Therapy in Action*

critique of the utilitarian perspective and the interpersonal and intra-personal viewpoints that are richly available in the film's contextual fabric. Clients may also be asked to look for comparative cases that may give rise to common points. For instance, the same movie may be compared with *The Wolf of Wall Street* (2013) in terms of the similarities of their display of a utilitarian and materialistic perspective and at the same time may be analyzed as to their underlying psychological threads on the concept of life and its delineation. Here the taxonomy would use both the comparison of the similar psychological elements in both films and would extract a more general feature that both films may tacitly imply.

3 **Films can entail and communicate psychological tools and psychological assumptions.** Films can provide a great array of topics where the psychological concepts and psychological constructs may be extracted and exemplified. Clients can be encouraged to watch given films and see how the content and the film ingredients may supply a wide repertoire of psychological topics. In watching a movie such as *The Awakening* (1980), viewers may be asked to inquire into the themes and concepts that may encompass a psychological potential to be examined. The pervasiveness of the medical model, the excavation of wellness, and the impact of doctors' relationship on patients' well-being may be presented in elaborating the film's psychological pieces. In *The Sound of Music* (1965), one may see how politics, love, yearning, and individual and social connection may come out of an interconnected cynosure of psychological belongings.

4 **Films relay polysemy in different levels.** Taking the film as a text, one may see the wide variety of multifarious levels of meaning in verbal, vocal, and visual levels. In *Phantom of the Opera* (1989), these levels marshal their presence in a wide variety of contexts. The surface and perfunctory dimensions of sensibility versus the profound structures come into being. The leap beyond the constructed conceptualization of beauty is delicately symbolized in sundry interactions. In *Cast Away* (2000), being alone and lonely produce their perlocutionary impact and bring forward the encounter with the identity away from the socially constructed manifestations. Clients can be invited to concentrate on locating the hermeneutics of meanings in manifold facets of a film.

5 **Films can bring a psychological combination of international, interdisciplinary, and intercultural considerations.** In movies such as *Lost in Translation* (2003), *Lion* (2016), *Ali's Wedding* (2017), and *My Big Fat Greek Wedding* (2002), the demonstration of the grammar of understanding in an intercultural context is pronounced, and clients can think over emotional triggers and their interconnectedness with cultural façade.

6 **Films can represent sociopolitical climate and can reflect the situational components of specific eras.** Clients may be instructed to delve into the

Film Therapy in Action   91

macro and microelements of a situation, an event, or an era and expound their dialectical relationships. *Dr. Zhivago* (1965) may be discussed and examined concerning the social and political climate of Russia. *Lawrence of Arabia* (1962) and *Lion of the Desert* (1981) may also be instantiated in illustrating the intricate potpourri of social and political configuration.

7 **Films can pertain to the scientific study of human behaviors, thoughts, and feelings.** Clients can be instructed to explore the psychological relationship between thoughts and feelings and thoughts and behaviors. In *Forest Gump* (1994), *The Notebook* (2004), *The Lion King* (1994) *The Da Vinci Code* (2006), and *A Walk to Remember* (2002), one may ponder the contour of an affective and cognitive network of operations. Clients can be led to identify feelings, emotions, and cognition and their implications for behaviors.

8 **Films can serve as prompts for signifying the significance of perspective.** A film can be a significant tool to help clients see the impact of perspective in determining the range of one's interpretation. In *The Prince and the Pauper* (1937), *A Christmas Carol* (2009), and *Hacksaw Ridge* (2016), clients can be invited to contemplate how a shift in perspective may develop a new horizon of possibility. They might also demonstrate how acting from one single perspective may give rise to mindlessness.

9 **Films can incorporate the significance of agency and responsibility.** *Endearment terms* may display how responsibility and devotion may unfold themselves as human virtues that can espouse novel changes and developments.

10 **Films can serve as an effective tool to encourage mindfulness.** *Scarlet Street* (1945), *Titanic* (1997), *The Wolf of Wall Street* (2013), *Midnight in Paris* (2011), *Glengarry Glen Ross* (1992), *The Scent of a Woman* (1992), and *I Am a Fugitive From a Chain Gang* (1932) all demonstrate numerous forms of mindlessness in a wide variety of contexts and can prompt numerous openings for a discussion of mindfulness as a way of being in the world.

11 **Films can display the significance of language in creating realities.** Different films from different eras and various genres can be explored in terms of their speech and psychological implications. *Les Misérables* (2012) is one of so many examples that may attenuate the formational and creational power of language in directing and creating powerful human effects.

12 **Films can take us to the function and mysteries of the unconscious.** To demonstrate the power of the unconscious and its penetrating power in human behavior, films can serve as a great tool to bring into the picture the effect and the implications of the unconscious. *Marnie* (1964) and *The Dark Past* (1948) are just two examples on a long list.

92   Film Therapy in Action

I Am a Fugitive From a Chain Gang (1932).

13 **Films can vividly demonstrate the panorama of a childlike world and its confrontation with the utilitarian world shrouded in consumerism and materialism.** *Bicycle Thief* (1948) can be discussed as a conspicuous example of delineating the beauty of a childlike world that may entail an infinite array of unspoken meanings in the context of human interactions.

14 **Films can signify the vitality of spirituality in the world of materialism.** Films can be psychologically assessed and analyzed by presenting the importance and impact of spirituality in human life. *The Wrong Man* (1956), *Contact* (1997), *We're No Angels* (1955), and *Les Misérables* (2012) are among films that can be psychologically examined in view of their psychological focus on spirituality.

Films may open up an extended possibility of revisiting thoughts, feelings, behaviors, and perspectives. They can be examined and discussed in terms of their explicit and implicit messages with their influencing vocal, visual, and verbal power. They can be taken into consideration as a whole.

In addition, parts of films can be addressed in connection with their messages, functionality, and impacts. Initially, a specific film can be selected based on the genre, tone, and plot to serve the therapy's objective. This selection may tend to highlight the importance of a topic in therapy, so a movie may be selected to explicate how bravery or gratitude, for instance, can elevate one's virtues. *Life of Pi* (2012) and *Hotel Rwanda* (2004) may be mentioned here as examples of movies focusing on bravery and courage. The therapeutic conversation may explore the topics to help the client experience critical thinking, metacognition, meta experience of emotions, and other intellectual and cognitive competencies.

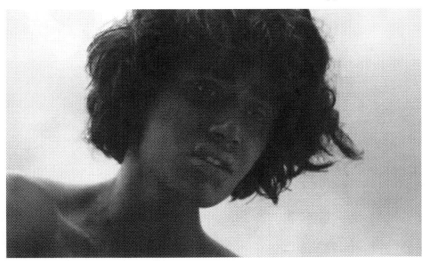

Life of Pi (2012).

On the other hand, a movie may be selected to underscore the role of emotions and their implications. Here, the emphasis is more on an elaborate concentration on the relationship between emotions and one's life and direction of the decision-making process. The discussions can then lead to the exploration of the client's real-life situations and the film's applications: what it is that the films offer for the client as a lesson to take away.

Movies such as *The Kid* (2019), *A Better Life* (2011), *On Golden Pond* (1981), *Harvey* (1950), and *The Blind Side* (2009) may be selected to exhibit the power of love as a positive emotion. They can be analyzed by their impact, applicability, and relationship to the client's situation.

An important point to reiterate is the discernment in the selection process of the movies. The movies need to be selected in view of the client's contextual situation, his or her ability to understand the complex layers in the given films, as well as age, education, cultural background, etc.

The therapeutic conversations regarding the specifically selected film can begin with an overview of the film while asking the client to present a precis of the story. The therapist can add and highlight extra materials to help the client present his or her summary of the film. The discussions can be followed by asking relevant questions based on the client's case. Some of the suggested questions and directions have been presented in previous chapters.

A further move would start by examining the lessons that can be taken away from the film in relation to the client's personal life.

The movie can be further documented to help the client reflect on the film's inspirational or insightful aspects. The therapist can help the client

94 *Film Therapy in Action*

see how there can be metaphoric relationships between a film and the client's identity: As movies open up their stories, clients have their own narratives. The unfolding aspect of the narrative can shape the client's identity. As movies have sequences and stages with their allusions to events and happenings, clients' narratives suggest what the clients have experienced and what they have gone through. As movies bring about a chain and an order in displaying what comes first and what comes next, clients' narratives also clarify how clients have viewed their lives, what may be missing, and what can constitute their points of accomplishment.

Inviting clients to see the role of choice, awareness, and creativity in the decision-making process, therapists can help clients see how different scenes may be restructured, reconstructed, decomposed, and recomposed. This may involve an engaging conversation of the emotional, behavioral, and cognitive dimensions of specific scenes in the film or the film's general view.

In reviewing the healthy versus unhealthy relationships in family life, for instance, the therapist may ask the client to view the film and see how contempt, criticism, defensiveness, and stonewalling may weaken the spirit of togetherness in family life and demoralize couples and children and reduce the psychological air in the family life. This may entail an in-depth discussion of Gottman's positivity ratio (see Gottman, 1994) or an examination of communication style, whether it is positive or negative, and its implications in relationship improvement or relationship destruction in Fredrickson's model (see Fredrickson & Losada, 2005).

12 Films, Politics, and Education

At first sight, politics, films, education, and therapy may not be related to one another since they each seem to have their own independent status. On the other hand, a macro analysis may help us understand how they may be connected to a discourse that may prescribe specific ideological engagements and promote certain models for dealing with life problems, problems of well-being, and challenges of specific eras.

Films may be used to describe, discuss, and examine the interplay of politics and the social construction of reality. The following quotes from the movie *All the President's Men* (1976) may portray how films may be contextualized to broaden the client's perspective in terms of metacognition, social awareness, relationship awareness, political awareness, and social and educational awareness:

DEEP THROAT: [*angry tone*] You let Haldeman slip away.

BOB WOODWARD: Yes.

DEEP THROAT: You've done worse than let Haldeman slip away: you've got people feeling sorry for him. I didn't think that was possible. In a conspiracy like this, you build from the outer edges and go step by step. If you shoot too high and miss, everybody feels more secure. You've put the investigation back months.

BOB WOODWARD: Yes, we know that. And if we're wrong, we're resigning. Were we wrong?

Movies such as *The Parallax View* (1974), *The Domino Principle* (1977), *Winter Kills* (1979), *Rocky* (1976), *Star Wars* (2017), *Close Encounters of the Third Kind* (1977), *Superman* (1987), *Dirty Harry* (1971), and *The French Connection* (1975) entail a complex set of levels that are rooted in macro and micro interactions. They decipher an extension of individual and social factors that are themselves tied to the hegemony of ideas, thoughts, and power plays in the structural levels of human interaction.

The following quotes from the movie *The French Connection* (1975) may be discussed in terms of their relationship in their embedded social structures.

DOI: 10.4324/9780429441431-12

96 *Films, Politics, and Education*

Rocky (1976).

WALT SIMONSON: Brooklyn is loaded with guys that own candy stores, two cars, and like to go to nightclubs!
BUDDY "CLOUDY" RUSSO: Yeah, but you put this little candy store hustler together with Joel Weinstock, and maybe we got a big score!
BUDDY "CLOUDY" RUSSO: He could have been white.
JIMMY "POPEYE" DOYLE: Never trust anyone!

Films may therefore facilitate the process of a critical discussion on political, social, and cultural issues. For instance, films may demonstrate how globalization and internationalization offer two different conceptualizations and bring about different implications. Globalization carries an ideological overture, whereas internationalization may bear upon a general sense of togetherness by removing barriers and frontiers.

Movies like *Super Size Me* (2004), *Rosetta* (1999), *Cathy Come Home* (1966), and *Selma* (2014) incorporate social, cultural, and political dimensions that broaden the perspective of the viewers toward the dialectical interplay of macro- and microcomponents of human life.

This might tend to support the role of films in expanding global education. While films may enhance the scope of intercultural awareness and international understanding, films need to be analyzed in terms of their subjugation to the pervasive ideological aspirations and hegemony of political and economic power at the utilitarian objectives' service.

In the movie *Night on Earth* (1991), the discourse of intercultural and interpersonal relationships is portrayed in connection with their affective and emotional signatures. The following quotes from the movie may point out how meanings are socially and interpersonally embedded within their individualized sphere of responsiveness:

VICTORIA SNELLING: What about marriage and a family?
CORKY: Definitely. I definitely want a family. Boys, though. Lots of boys.

Films, Politics, and Education 97

VICTORIA SNELLING: No girls? Girls are nice, too, I think.

CORKY: Ahhh, maybe some girls, too. But you know, like, that stuff, that's all besides the point. The real problem is to find a good guy for the father.

VICTORIA SNELLING: Tell me about it.

CORKY: Well. I'm real particular, you know? And I'm also patient enough. I mean, at least I hope I am. Cuz, you know, I don't know, maybe you got to wait a while, you know. Cuz maybe it's not so easy to find the exact right guy, you know? Like, the one guy, you know?

In what follows, I highlight how movies may also misrepresent cultural, social, and political dimensions of human life and may embark on distorting people's lived experiences. To do that, I address the concept of globalization and its call for educational expansion. The point is to critique the concept of global education and demonstrate how films may advocate or critique the globalization of education and its political implications.

Global education is a term with complementary associations. Its acclamation has been coupled with its claims of enlightenment, illumination, improvement, progress, cultural awareness, appreciation of diversity, human rights awareness, global knowledge, and global change (see, for instance, Anderson, 1979; Hanvey, 1976; Merryfield, 1997, 2009,; Tucker, 2009). Respect for others, listening to other voices, appreciation of cultural diversity, openness toward learning from other cultures, and recognizing the rights of other groups and people who may have been marginalized, underrepresented, or misrepresented are at the forefront of the proglobal education campaign (see, for instance, Case, 1993; Coombs, 1989).

While global education can offer promising chapters in affecting the quality of life of both educators and the educated, it needs to be mindfully deconstructed in order to present practical solutions for global challenges. In line with this deconstruction, certain layers appear to be of first and foremost excavation.

The roots of global education are mainly embedded within the political conditions after World War II. These conditions seem to have contributed to the emergence of global thinking about several issues, including education. The United States membership in UNESCO, the approval of the Fulbright Act with a focus on the exchange of students around the world, passing the National Defense Education Act in the United States, and its call for funding foreign languages and studies on foreign cultures as a response to the Soviet Union's launching of Sputnik, the first man-made space satellite, are all examples of conditions that gave rise to thinking about global education. Organizations such as American Forum for Global Education, Education for a World in Change, and the Study Commission on Global Education have accordingly appeared in the contextual flow of political conditions (Tucker, 2009).

98   *Films, Politics, and Education*

Understanding the underlying political factors and components of global education would elucidate that global education did not emerge as an independent philosophical enterprise within the Westernized discourse of education. Global education did not present itself as a utopian constituent of a worldview on human beings where education had to be a significant pillar of recognition. Global education thus was not created within an ontological system of a worldview that encouraged and promoted education as a value system. The "ought" of global education, in other words, did not extract its implications from the "is" of a philosophical project with a mission for human beings; it came mainly as a response or a reaction to conditions and situational analyses that induced thinking globally about education. Underneath this reaction, there were sedimentations of fear, the hysteria of the cold war, the anxiety of losing the competitive game, and the fervor for superiority. Therefore, the global education discourse was not a creative and proactive discourse of its own within the Westernized worldview on education. This is not to downgrade the positive effects of global education but to illustrate the necessity of reflecting on the possibility of thinking independently about global education. An independent project on global education needs to address the following questions:

1   Is global education inherently defined in utilitarianism's etiological patterns, or is it embedded within a spiritual and transcendental mission? The implications of each would bring about practical involvements and sensitive engagements with opposing and paradoxical programs. Think about a global education program with a utilitarian focus to understand the children or the war-torn situation in Iraq and Afghanistan. A global education in pursuit of clandestinely defined profits at a local level, albeit a global–local, would fail. On numerous manifestations of this failure, Spariosu (2004) wrote:
    Whether on the right or the left, our global pundits seem to connect human progress primarily with material development. Most worldwide statistics and indicators are economic in nature, measuring human happiness by what an individual or a social group has, rather than by what they are. Thus, we have presently divided the world into "developed," "underdeveloped," and "developing" societies. But if we truly wish to change our global paradigms, then we need to change the focus of our worldwide efforts from social and economic development to human self-development. From the latter's standpoint, there are no developed or underdeveloped societies, but only developing ones. It is this kind of development that, in the end, will help us solve our practical problems, including world hunger, poverty, and violence, and will turn the earth into a welcoming and nurturing home for all of its inhabitants, human and nonhuman. (p. 5)

Films, Politics, and Education 99

2 How does global education define human beings? Can we really do global education without spelling out very clearly what we mean by being and becoming a human? Does global education serve as a program for humanity, or is it a prescriptive program that endorses certain privileged groups? If the former tends to be the case, what are the underlying constituents of a project on humanity? If the latter turns out to be the goal, what are the sources of legitimacy? Is the global connection elicited from common human bonds, or is it taken from special groups' interests?

Suppose global education tends to proceed with an evolutionary Darwinian viewpoint and its definition of human beings. In that case, it cannot downplay acknowledging that certain groups should perish since they cannot cope with the changes. Global education, therefore, is to engage in a profound ontological and epistemological deconstruction: What is knowing and what is the meaning of being? What is learning about? Is learning a process of producing automatons, or is it a process of liberation? How do knowing and interacting with one another? Where does humanity stand in the project? What does a student in North America need to know about his or her being and its connection to other beings? Is he or she considered a knower only if he or she has access to certain modes of knowing? What if the circle of knowing excludes certain ways of knowing and encourages special ways of knowing? How does the definition of humanity affect the search for knowing? Is the sphere of *being* bound by the empirically established categories and propositions? If yes, how does that sphere include and exclude the claims of global education and global project? Suppose the children in Islamabad, Tehran, Cairo, and Bangladesh are exposed to presentations that give credit to nonempirical and nonpositivist observations. Does that make sense to a global education that has nullified nonempirical observations? How can a child in North America get a sense of education of, let's say, Afghanistan children if the North American child is only exposed to pervasive Westernized discourses?

Suppose the documentaries that report the status of education cite Taliban as the representation of Islam and Taliban's emphasis on preventing females from attending schools. How does that image correspond to the world of Islam where Muslims quoting the prophet Mohammad claim that seeking to know and learning would be incumbent upon both males and females?

If the community of learners is infused with numerous forms of politically based information, does that promote a truly global education?

3 How does global education address the gaps between signs and meanings? A sign is a combination of both signifier and signified. The signifier is an image or a sound that refers to a concept. The signified is the concept to which the signifier is referring to. Let's say that I ask

100 *Films, Politics, and Education*

you any of the following questions: How is your mom doing? How is your mother doing? How is your ma doing? How is your mommy doing? I have used different signs with some similarities and some differences. Nonetheless, the meaning of a mother is going to be different for the recipients of the message. If you have experienced a very emotional attachment to your mother, the meaning would be way different for you in comparison with someone who can think of his or her mother only as the one who carried him or her for just under a year. Global education is brim with signs. The meanings, however, need to be explored and examined not through the lenses of the core references but through the marginal, associative, affective, and emotional reference points. To exemplify, Iranian-based curriculum on both the elementary and secondary levels has a huge emphasis on metacognition in classes such as language arts and social studies. The curriculum may appear to be esoteric, insensible, and unrelated for an educator not familiar with the cultural styles and cognitive styles behind those meta cognition prompts.

A study by Osunde et al. (1996) indicated that lack of accessibility to the deep layers of understanding others from a different culture brings about clichés and stereotyped knowing that work against the true nature of global education. In their study, they focused on how preservice social studies teachers perceived Africa. In their study of 100 preservice teachers from the United States, Osunde et al. (1996) found that the majority of the concepts associated with Africa were nothing but tigers, disease, jungles, poor, deserts, and superstition. Osunde et al. (1996) demonstrated how the American preservice teachers' exposure to signs (as indicated above) prevents them from understanding the deep layers of meaning-making about Africa. They indicated that

> Even though preservice teachers are exposed to an increasing amount of information on Africa through their college courses and seminars, and even though the media now presents news on Africa with more frequency, the results of our data analysis showed that a majority of the preservice social studies teachers had the same misconceptions about Africa that their grandparents and parents had several decades ago.
>
> (p. 120, cited in Tucker, 2009)

In line with this attempt, Spariosu (2004) focuses on ways and strategies that can bring about a "global mindset" for fostering a truly global education. He brings numerous examples from Rumi, Abu Sa'id, Shabestari, and others as "an expression of the same nonlinear, irenic way of thinking in the Islamic tradition" to elucidate the significance of thinking that lies outside the Western civilization. (Spariosu, 2004, p. 133)

Films, Politics, and Education 101

His arguments on establishing a real engagement with a concentration on multilateral teamwork and intercultural and transdisciplinary dialogue would facilitate the process of identifying non-Western educational approaches. These approaches may be easily concealed to oblivion because of the pervasive discourses within the Western educational system.

A global education that is entrenched within one single perspective would lead to mindlessness that ignores and discounts other perspectives.

Langer (1997) encouraged a mindful disengagement from remaining in a single perspective and exploring alternative ways of looking and says:

> In a mindful state, we implicitly recognize that no one perspective optimally explains a situation. Therefore, we do not seek to select the one response that corresponds to the situation, but we recognize that there is more than one perspective on the information given, and we choose from among these.
>
> (p. 108)

Deep within the underlying elements of global education, its conceptualization, planning, policies, and proposals lay a claim of authority and ownership. To put it differently, global education is strongly embedded within the assumptions of power and authority in that education needs to be done globally but by virtue of leadership that not only gives direction to how and what of the movement but also decides on the sources that endorse or refute the legitimacy of inclusion, sensibility, and expressiveness of others. The discourse of power itself emanates from a potpourri of political and economic factors with a strong propensity toward superiority. The establishment of the claim of authority and ownership can play a huge destructive role in the true nature of global education as it imposes narrow-mindedness and parochialism on a wide variety of levels; it sanctions against inclusionary, it impedes the process of a real understanding, and it censures a profound deconstruction of the politically and economically established assumptions. Huntington's assumptions, for instance, have widened the gap between the West and the East. Global education's hubris with the ownership takes an expansionist view that marginalizes learning and dialogue about others and projects a series of assumptions and perceptions upon the world.

Building upon Willinsky (1998), Merryfield (2009) illustrated how imperialism and the imperialist way of thinking can influence global education with specific political and economic ambitions. She reminded us how the discourse of power within the imperialist design of education can highlight one thing's grandeur and downgrade the other thing. On this analysis, Merryfield (2009) wrote:

> Whether the dichotomous terms are The Orient/The occident, First World/Third World, free/communist, or industrialized/developing nations, there is an "us"—usually the white middle-class descendants

102 *Films, Politics, and Education*

of Western Europeans who are said to have developed democracy and today make the world safe—and "them," the Others who are divided from real Americans by their culture, skin color, language, politics, or other differences.

(p. 219)

The claim for ownership and authority for global education is associated with the emergence of privileged status with certain goals. If global education's etiological definition is summed up in reductionism, materialism, and a positivist and linear way of thinking about the subject matter of global education, namely, human beings, the privilege will be designated and assigned to the voices that would substantiate the utilitarian project. How can global education offer an in-depth understanding of intercultural relationships if it is encapsulated and circumscribed by a culture of reductionism? If voices need to be expressed on the strength of global education discourse of sensibility, how can global education provide a practically opulent dialogue among cultures?

The claim of ownership and authority is largely indebted to the technological advancement in numerous stages, the natural sciences' salient leaps of progress, and the rapid growth of information and communication technology. This can have several adverse effects in a proactive global education: (a) It can generate a huge emphasis on accessing the technique at the peril of ignoring the ethical values. The notion that an increase of computers in classrooms would give rise to a growth in understanding is an example of such an emphasis. (b) It can impose a machine-oriented perspective on human beings. This perspective would lead to a metaphor where the subject matter of global education, namely, human beings, would be equal to automatons. You may cry beside a computer, tell the funniest jokes, read the most beautiful poems, show the scenes of human massacre, or explicate the values of devotion and benevolence; what does the computer do? A machine-oriented perspective would have no room for promoting global responsibility. (c) Global education, in its present form, can easily neglect and ignore voices that fall outside the discourses of linear and positivist thinking. I shall explain one example of negligence or ignorance in the context of discussions on global education. Huntington (1996) tried to indicate that Islam is inherently tied to violence and violent actions are ineluctably linked to the Islamic perspective. With a very basic understanding of the Islamic worldview, one can easily identify the frivolousness of Huntington's statements. Examining the Islamic perspective on the rights of human beings and the significance of comprehensive respect of human rights, Jafari, an Iranian contemporary philosopher and scholar of Islam, (2006) cited Imam Ali of Muslims with the following decrees on the rights of animals:

Do not keep the animals and their children separate from one another.

Make sure that you keep your nails short upon milking lest the animals may feel annoyed.

Films, Politics, and Education   103

If you happen to take the animals out for grazing, make sure that you walk them through the beautiful meadows if there are any.

Rest assured that enough milk is left for the animal when milking.

God will damn the one who uses profane language while addressing any animal.

The governor can punish anyone who does not take care of his/her animal.
(pp. 159–162)

Jafari (2004, 2006) then asked how a worldview that is so sensitive to the rights of animals can be indifferent when dealing with human rights and global education. He cited numerous examples within the Islamic tradition to argue that Islam displays an essentially vital sensitivity toward any living creature's rights with the maximum possible rights for any human being.

Huntington's allegations have been strongly refuted even in the West by those with a very basic understanding of Islam. On "the insidiousness of Huntington's arguments," Spariosu (2004) wrote:

The traditional greeting among Muslims is "Peace be with you" (Al-Salam Alei-kum) or that Sufi teachings do not condone violence and conflict any more than their Buddhist, Taoist, or Christian counterparts do. For example, the prophet Muhammad says: "If a man gives up quarreling when he is in the wrong, a house will be built for him in Paradise. But if a man gives up a conflict even when he is in the right, a house will be built for him in the loftiest of Paradise" (Frager and Fadiman 1997, p. 84). If anything, Huntington's and Payne's arguments highlight the ignorance of even-well trained Westerners about other cultures and religions (not to mention their own) and the urgent need for educating the world's youth about each other's—and their own—cultural traditions.

(p. 51)

Hakimi, another Iranian philosopher and scholar of Islam (2004), presented an in-depth analysis on the word "Islam" and prophet Muhammad on the strength of a series of evidence within Islamic tradition and argued that prophet Muhammad serves as the source of mercy, peace, and compassion for the whole universe. In citing numerous pieces of evidence, he recounted the story of prophet Muhammad, who comes under the frequent daily attack of an assailant who even throws the bladder of a sheep at the prophet. The prophet pays a visit to the man once he receives the news of his illness.

Having read the above examples, one may reflect on how a learner in North America may be subscribed to a single perspective that would be drastically different from the original culture.

104 *Films, Politics, and Education*

Global education needs to disclaim its belonging to merely Westernized discourse of power and its politically established agenda. It needs to extend the possibility of connection to the peripheral and the marginal voices, to the visible and the invisible players, to the represented, under-represented, and misrepresented. Global education needs to offer the possibility of a collaboration among the world's people, so they construct knowledge through their contribution and participation, not that they be given the knowledge through the privileged. Global education needs to disavow its belonging to political agenda that moves in line with some political leaders' interests. In the words of Spariosu (2004), "So, it is neither Islam nor the West that are a problem for each other, but certain political leaders and their advisers" (p. 52).

Spariosu (2004) considered the practical key to promoting global education as the implementation of major reforms within the higher education system, particularly in the universities. He argued that educational institutions overwhelmed by red tape and bureaucratic systems would act as obstacles in the way of true global education. Such institutions, he further claimed, develop entanglements in the face of real participative measures and global education. He argued that

> In attempting to reorient the university toward global education, let alone global intelligence, we come up against what seems to be insurmountable obstacles because the very academic place that has traditionally been designed to address important social and human problems seems to compound, rather than to alleviate, such problems. As we have seen, many of our educational institutions have simply become reflections of global predicaments instead of active leaders out of such predicaments. For instance, at most U.S. universities, current administrators, despite paying lip service to the "internationalization of the curriculum," often perceive study abroad and experiential education as expensive extras that interrupt students' normal campus activities. To make matters worse, the academic credit systems that are currently in place at most North American Universities are highly protectionist. Through time-and energy-consuming bureaucratic red tape, they make it deliberately difficult for students to move across disciplines and higher learning institutions both in the United States and overseas.
>
> (Spariosu, 2004, p. 200)

Said's *Orientalism* (1978), *Culture and Imperialism* (1993), and *Covering Islam* (1997) demonstrate how Western education is entangled with a hegemonic discourse that gives superiority, authority, and ownership to certain groups, namely, Europeans. Said (1978) argued that colonizers considered themselves not only the possessors of knowledge, expertise, and education but also the source of privileges that bestowed them with the right to define others. He indicated that education driven by colonization

Films, Politics, and Education 105

and oppressors controlled the construction of the interaction among identity, power, language, education, and knowing. Such an education, Said argued, imposed certain prescriptions against the oppressed and the exploited.

Said's arguments in _Culture and Imperialism_ (1993) depict how the discourse of oppression and power clandestinely and extensively infiltrated the realm of not only the cognition but also emotions and behavior: The oppressed had to see the world through the glasses of the oppressors and those colonized had to abide by the mindset and the culture of the colonizers, the exploited had to choose the choice of words of the exploiters, the deprived had to express themselves in accordance with the standards set by the oppressors. The oppressors had the privilege of defining the right and the wrong: they had the ownership of everything.

The sedimentation of the imperialist way of thinking allows Western global education a claim that can justify quintessential supervision for decision making, diagnosis, and intervention in the realm of education. The entrapment of global education within the ideologically and economically driven globalization would hinder the process of global education as a movement that can promote global citizenship.

Freire's _Pedagogy of Freedom_ (1998a) and _Pedagogy of the Oppressed_ (1998b) critically delineate the dangers of an economically driven global education and encourage awareness of a real collaboration among the educators and learners so they can critically examine the creation and construction of knowledge. Such construction of knowledge, Freire argued, needs to be liberated from the subjugation of those who grandiloquently consider themselves as the owner of knowing.

For global education to be globally effective, it needs to revisit the plethora of forces that have explicated global education's claim and totalitarian tyranny. This can produce huge implications for addressing the situations and conditions of those not affiliated with the privileged voices. An authentic global education needs to allow everyone to critically elucidate and analyze the input and output of the so-called global education establishments and organizations. Such an analytical approach would involve not only the interests of the citizens of wealthy countries that happen to be the members of the organizations but also the interests of the non-members that can contribute to global education to achieve a globally sustainable peace and development.

In line with this revisiting, the Organization for Economic Cooperation and Development (OECD), the Program for International Student Assessment (PISA), the World Trade Organization (W.T.O.), the United Nation's Conference of Trade and Development (UNCTAD), and so many other organizations and programs can be encouraged to explore the possibility of a shift of attention from political leaders' presumptions of education to a comprehensive inclusion of others who may have been fully concealed to oblivion through the ownership of global education. The

106 *Films, Politics, and Education*

shift can bring to light the multiplicities and fragments that have been put aside in the galloping trend of the reductionist materialism of global education. The shift can also illustrate the significance of an engagement with the practical intercultural strategies that help implement an effective global education management program.

If global education is incarcerated within the power of politics and its ramifications, how can it foster global citizenship? In order for global education to harbor global citizenship, global education needs to be emancipated from the manacles of politically based parochialism that circumscribe the open and comprehensive activities of global education. Global citizenship requires the involvement and active participation of everyone globally; it necessitates an active engagement on the part of everyone. How can a participative involvement transpire if the discourse of power has already established contingencies that hamper the presence of others who do not move in line with the rules of the games within the hegemonic discourse of power and its utilitarian domination?

Questioning and critiquing the paradigms that define global action and infuse globalization, Gills (2002) argued that

> There has been much discussion of the so called nonstate actors and the rise and importance of non-governmental organizations and other international societal factors in recent years of globalization. Yet, we can observe for ourselves how it is still the most powerful governments of the world that determine the primary course of action and define the parameters of mainstream discussion whenever there is a crisis. Thus, the world order's embedded power structure has been highlighted even in the so-called era of globalization. Nevertheless, if we look deeper, we can see things differently, and we may realize the potential for positive change. Rather than accepting the still reigning paradigm of (past) international relations, with its enduring feature of governance by a few great powers based on their ability to use military force, we must urgently look for ways to turn to a positive alternative.

> (p. 159)

If globalization is politically tied to global education focusing on particular voices, how can it truly listen to other voices? Global education inspired by political globalization would develop a monological and not a dialogical relationship where citizens receive prescriptions before they can get any diagnosis.

Challenging such globalization and its outcry for subjugation, Spariosu (2004) mindfully examined Huntington's perniciously destructive analysis and stated that

> if Huntington's history teaches us anything, it is that power has often fared best under various disguises, rather than through raw display,

Films, Politics, and Education 107

that is, that soft power can often be harder than hard power. This truth should be painfully obvious to those U.S. foreign policymakers who advocate preemptive strikes as a way of preventing terrorist and other military activities on the part of so-called rogue nations and political groups, inimical to the United States and its closest allies. Such displays of raw power have led, for example, to the current debacle in the Middle East.

(p. 55)

The concept of citizenship, ipso facto, is a Western-oriented concept with its roots in liberalism, the classical ideas of democracy and participation in the *polis* of ancient Greece, and entitlement within northern Italy's autonomous cities (Turner, 1993). If global education's global citizenship is positioned within the circumscribing discourse of the West, how can it bring involvement from everyone? Furthermore, if global education fails to study other countries' global education experiences, how can it enter a global dialogue to invite everyone's contribution?

Global education's present literature is rife with works within the Western discourse of education and hardly has serious inclusion of any works from the other parts of the world. Interesting and ironically enough, Hakimi (2004) and Jafari (2006) presented evidence that indicates the engagements of some Muslim scholars with both global education and internationalization of education. They argued that the Islamic worldview does not belong to geography or a place and therefore addresses the common ties among human beings in explicating a message that is not bound by one nation or a group. Both Hakimi (2002) and Jafari (2006) claimed that an Islamic ontology is in pursuit of bringing education for everyone in the world as it has a special focus on human beings' togetherness. Hakimi (2002) cited Imam Ali, saying that there is not even one single action, neither minor nor major, whereupon one is in dire need of understanding and awareness. He proposed a global Islamic perspective on education where everyone feels connected and tied to the others in the world. This connection can be further strengthened through a mindful involvement for implementing peace and mercy not only in small and interconnected communicates but also in larger worldwide networks.

The present literature on global education seldom reflects any such propositions as the assumptions promoted by Huntington and Lewis bring forth fear and negativity and not hope and optimism. In delineating this fear, Said (1978, 1993, 1997) wrote,

As I suggest, European interest in Islam derived not from curiosity but from fear of a monotheistic, culturally, and militarily formidable competitor to Christianity. As numerous historians have shown, the earliest European scholars of Islam were medieval polemicists writing to ward off the threat to Muslim hordes and apostasy. In one way or another, that combination of fear and hostility has persisted to the

108 *Films, Politics, and Education*

present day, both in scholarly and non-scholarly attention to an Islam which is viewed as belonging to a part of the world—the Orient—counterposed imaginatively, geographically, and historically against Europe and the West.

(p. 344)

Global education needs to choose a different language, a different discourse, and a new approach toward examining, discussing, and presenting issues in the global world. It needs to openly listen to others without imposing a selective process for listening. In doing this, the discourse of superiority needs to be replaced with a shift in listening, thinking, and analyzing. Global education's mindset needs to be liberated from the yoke of the poisonous emotions and feelings that dictate coercive and manipulative decision-making.

In explaining the flux of such implications, Said (2003) indicated:

There has been so massive and calculatedly aggressive attack on the contemporary societies of the Arab and Muslim for their backwardness, lack of democracy, and abrogation of women's rights that we simply forget that such notions as modernity, enlightenment, and democracy are by no means simple and agreed upon concepts that one wither does or does not find, like Easter eggs in the living-room. The breathtaking insouciance of jejune publicists who speak in the name of foreign policy and who have no living notion (or any knowledge at all) of the language of what real people actually speak has fabricated an arid landscape ready for American power to construct there an ersatz model of the free market "democracy," without even a trace of doubt that such projects don't exist outside of Swift's Academy of Lagado.

(p. xiv)

For global education to take a new stance, it needs to revisit human beings' definition and the common denominators of being a human being. The current language of violence as conspicuously exhibited by mass media needs to be fundamentally transformed into a language of peace not just at perfunctory levels but in profound demonstrations of peaceful structures. The current news coverage is drastically deleterious, violent, and destructive. What do citizens of the world learn when they are extensively and frequently exposed to annihilating fashions of conflicts, skirmishes, and encounters? If global education tacitly gets stratified within the discourse of antagonism, how can global education serve as a source for composure? Suppose the culture of violence and threat serves to be persistently viable and pervasive. How can global education promise the possibility of celebrating global citizenship where empathy and comfort stand at the threshold of its commencement? How can global education offer the panacea of solidarity and togetherness when the citizens of the world feel inextricably enslaved by a seemingly insurmountable culture of alienation

Films, Politics, and Education   109

and separation? As the etymology of both "whole" and "health" suggests, the detachment from the whole works against the health process. A fragmented global education with political egoism and egotism would block the exploratory journey of learning from the *whole* where each part needs to be fully recognized as a complementary phase of the project and not in contraposition to the others.

Global education needs to be connected to global wisdom where the heart and mind walk arm in arm and not against one another, where the roots are allowed to stand outright by the appearances, where the multiplicity of thinking can open up the possibility of consensus. Global education inspired by global wisdom looks for human freedom from modern slavery that is not unlike the old slavery in nature. Global education driven by a pearl of global wisdom calls on cultures to borrow from one another, share their experienced individuality, and become united to affect the quality of life beyond the quotidian stratum of consumerism and materialism. Global education intertwined with global wisdom would substantiate the pearl of living together through peace and understanding away from manufacturing solipsism.

The first move toward this possibility begins with the courage to challenge the insinuations that defy and denounce the wisdom that would reveal the nakedness of global education: a mischievous kid may help us see the captivity of the crowd and their infatuation with the surface.

Keeping in mind the importance of films in constructing realities, therapists may bear in mind that their film selections and their guiding frameworks need to go beyond the superficial and perfunctory levels of understanding. To put it simply, therapists may be subjected to the hegemony of a discourse of legitimacy and privilege that may prescribe certain position-taking and specific approaches in dealing with people's problems and challenges.

This may be intertwined with a root analysis of the pervasive perspectives on the mission of psychology.

Latour (2004) noted that

> Only in the name of science is Stanley Milgram's experiment possible, to take one of Stengers and Despret's topoi. In any other situation, the students would have punched Milgram in the face, thus displaying a very sturdy and widely understood disobedience to authority. Those students went along with Milgram's torture does not prove they harbored some built-in tendency to violence but demonstrates only the capacity of scientists to produce artifacts no other authority can manage to obtain because they are undetectable.
>
> The proof of this is that Milgram died, not realizing that his experiment had proven nothing about average American inner tendency to obey—except that they could give the appearance of obeying white coats! Yes, artifacts can be obtained in the name of science, but

110   *Films, Politics, and Education*

this is not itself a scientific result. It is a consequence of the way science is handled (see the remarkable case of Glickman 2000).

(p. 222)

In elaborating psychological perspectives' reliance on the hegemony of the political power, Teo (2005) wrote:

Psychology has been transformed from a philosophical into a natural scientific discipline on the background of colonialism, slavery, and exploitation. Thus, it is not surprising that important pioneers of psychology assimilated or actively contributed to scientific racism. Paul Broca (1824–1880), who is celebrated in psychology for his location of speech loss (aphasia) in an area of the brain (known as Broca's area), was one of the leaders of scientific racism. He was convinced that non-European races were inferior in terms of intelligence, vigor, and beauty (see Teo 2005). It is also remarkable that Broca gave up all standards of scientific inquiry when he "handled" research on human "races." At the beginning were his conclusions, which were followed by data collection and selective reports. Criteria were changed and abandoned when the results did not fit his original conclusions (see Gould 1996). He embraced "confirming" evidence and repressed disconfirming information. The pioneer of social psychology Gustave Le Bon (1841–1931), who divided, based on psychological criteria, humans into primitive, inferior, average, and superior races, suggested vehemently that races were physiologically and psychologically distinct, that races were different species, and that all members of a race shared an immutable race soul (see Teo 2005).

(pp. 154–157)

The point here is to demonstrate how films can counteract what the films have been sometimes exploited to do. In other words, films may serve as a subtle and artistic tool to manipulate people's minds and may promote specific directed programs of utilitarianism and consumerism.

Pretty Woman (1990) is a movie that promotes and portrays consumerism and materialism while focusing on *having* as a sign of privilege. In other words, the film underscores that one's credibility, one's status, and one's privilege are inextricably tied to one's possessions and one's material belongings. Money brings glory and happiness in the context of the movie.

The following quotes from the movie may delineate how the film's interactions and conversations are embedded within a materialistic framework.

KIT: I don't know. Maybe you could, like, buy a horse and some diamonds.
EDWARD LEWIS: How much for the entire night?
VIVIAN: Stay here? You couldn't afford it.

EDWARD LEWIS: Try me.
VIVIAN: 300 dollars.

The in-depth analysis of the conversations mentioned above may demonstrate how consumerism, materialism, and their generative ideology may describe the natural life as a life interwoven with a desire to the consumer, an eagerness to possess, and a willingness to indulge in a materialistic competition.

In describing the consumeristic modern world, Steven Miles (1998) argued that

> Consumerism appears to have become part and parcel of the very fabric of modern life. Areas of social life that were previously free of the demands of the marketplace have had to adapt to a world where the needs and desires of the consumer are apparently paramount. How we consume, why we consume, and the parameters laid down for us within which we consume have become increasingiy significant influences on how we construct our everyday lives.
>
> (p. 1)

It is important that therapists enhance their spectrum of knowledge on the relationship between films and politics and education and see how their choices of films and the representations of the films' contents are linked to ideology and culture.

Therapists may use films to help general clients gain social knowledge and get oriented toward multidimensional aspects of emotions in films.

Movies including *American Psycho* (2000), *Fight Club* (1999), and *Clueless* (1995) demonstrate the power of consumerism and materialism in people's lives. The critique of consumerism may also be noticeable in other movies such as *Glengarry Glen Ross* (1992). The movie depicts how money, power, consumerism, and materialism are interlocked in people's lives: people's thinking, feelings, behaviors, and destiny, in general, are subjected to the interplay of material forces that limit, contain, and circumscribe people's domain of actions and freedom.

Likewise, the following monologue in the movie *Fight Club* (1999) may demonstrate how identity, consumerism, and materialism are inseparably tied together:

> Like so many others, I had become a slave to the IKEA nesting instinct ... when I saw something clever like a coffee table in the shape of a yin-yang, I had to have it ... lamps of environmentally friendly unbleached paper; I'd flip through catalogs and wonder what dining set defines me as a person. I had it all. Even the glass dishes with tiny bubbles and imperfections; proof that they were crafted by the honest, simple, hardworking, indigenous peoples of wherever.

112 *Films, Politics, and Education*

The poignancy of a life without meaning in the world of consumerism is depicted in the movies mentioned above, where the constant tendency to buy and consume is considered natural.

Having in mind a critical view on developing social awareness, therapists may engage themselves and their clients in pondering the following questions:

1 What is the role of movies in illustrating an ontological perspective: what exists and what does not? Is existence merely bound in the material world, or may there be other layers of existence?
2 How do certain movies demonstrate the power of ideology and culture in constructing realities of life?
3 How do certain movies display a world of values in the context of materialism and consumerism?
4 How do certain movies facilitate social, political, economic, and cultural understandings of our world?
5 How do certain movies emphasize or marginalize values?
6 How do certain movies prescribe, promote, and endorse certain ways of living?
7 How do movies promote and educate concepts, ideas, attitudes, and values?
8 How do movies persuade people?
9 How do movies deal with questions of racism, multiculturalism, poverty, social justice, and discrimination?

The Life of Emile Zola (1937).

Films, Politics, and Education   113

10 How do movies present politics and culture?
11 How can movies educate clients on the interplay of politics and education?
12 How can movies educate clients on the interplay of cinema and politics?
13 How can movies develop a broader understanding of global problems?
14 How can movies give rise to a general awareness of global crises?

It is important to note that films may serve as a great tool to highlight social and political issues. *Dr. Zhivago* (1965), *The Hurricane* (1999), *I Am Fugitive From a Chain Gang* (1932), *Les Misérables* (2012), *J.F.K.* (1991), *Nixon* (1995), *The President* (2014), *The Wolf of Wall Street* (2013), and *The Life of Emile Zola* (1937) are among many films that may portray how politics, racism, heartlessness, tension, conflicts, greed, and injustice have destroyed people's lives.

13 Film and Poetry

Films and poetry share at least one common denominator: they represent human artistic and aesthetic composition and creation. Both films and poetry may entail evocative, provocative, insightful, illuminating, and enlightening moments of self-awareness, social awareness, and relationship awareness. Poetic discourse and film script represent human endeavor to fathom deep down the human mind and human heart to elucidate the dynamics of being and becoming, happiness and sadness, love and hatred, composure and pandemonium, trust and pessimism. Orson Welles once said, "A film is never really good unless the camera is an eye in the head of a poet."

Paterson (2016) exemplifies a movie with a focus on a week in the life of Paterson, a New Jersey bus driver who aspires to be a poet and embarks on writing poetry on a daily basis. He tries to examine beauty in everything around him and gives rise to a poetic composition by looking at mundane and banal things from a delicate and aesthetic perspective.

Other movies including *The Nightmare Before Christmas* (2020), *Poetry* (2010), *O Brother, Where Art Thou?* (2000) *Howl* (2015), *Bright Star* (2009), *The Basketball Diaries* (1995), and *Dead Poets Society* (1989) bring poetic overture into their content either by focusing on a poet's poetic expressiveness or by delineating the impact of poetry and teaching people how to live poetically in the world.

The following quotes from the movie *Dead Poets Society* (1989) might reveal the tone and diction of poetic spirit and its manifestation in one's phenomenological way of living:

JOHN KEATING: No matter what anybody tells you, words and ideas can change the world.

In line with a demonstration of an interest in revisiting life's questions, the movie tends to focus on an emphasis of a detachment from hackneyed layers of life, routinized behavior, and mundane complexions of our interactions. The following exchange in the film might present a depiction of this sort.

DOI: 10.4324/9780429441431-13

Film and Poetry 115

NEIL: I went into the woods because I wanted to live deliberately. I wanted to live deep and suck out all the marrow of life to put to rout all that was not life, and not, when I came to die, discover that I had not lived.

MCALLISTER: Show me the heart unfettered by foolish dreams, and I'll show you a happy man!

The movie also proceeds with an exposition of the significance of self-discovery, finding out one's voice, and becoming oriented toward one's role and responsibility in deciding one's direction.

John Keating's words below elucidate the predilection toward self-discovery:

JOHN KEATING: Boys, you must strive to find your own voice. Because the longer you wait to begin, the less likely you are to find it at all. Thoreau said, "Most men lead lives of quiet desperation." Don't be resigned to that. Break out!Underscoring the uniqueness of voice for everyone, John calls for challenging the peer group pressure and conformity. His emphasis explicates the role of self-confidence in finding the path and illustrates this by saying the following:

JOHN KEATING: Now we all have a great need for acceptance, but you must trust that your beliefs are unique, your own, even though others may think them odd or unpopular, even though the herd may go, "that's b - - a - - d." Robert Frost said, "Two roads diverged in the wood and I, I took the one less traveled by, and that has made all the difference.'

A wide variety of movies entail poetry. Epic poems are noticeable in some movies, such as *Troy* (2004), *The Raven* (2012), *Beowulf* (2007), *Mulan* (2020), *and Braveheart* (1995). Poetry displays its presence in films about poets such as Shakespeare in *Shakespeare in Love* (1998), T.S. Eliot in *Tom & Viv* (1994) and *Sylvia Plath* (2003), and Ted Hughes in *Sylvia* (1965). Poetry also displays its power in many movies in dramatic and unexpected ways.

Poetry offers a delicate and heartful language in describing, explicating, delineating, and analyzing events, phenomena, people, and perspectives. Poetry elevates a high sense of awareness and perspicacity through which a great discernment is brought into life and livelihood.

Movies with poetry point out a transcendental sense of belonging that incorporates both being and longing. They are being as the manifestation of an existential status with a particular manifestation and longing as a constantly reverberating predilection to supersede the constriction of the bound form of being.

To Ricoeur (1991a), "It is the task of poetry to make words mean as much as they can and not as little as they can" (p. 449). Therefore, the

116   *Film and Poetry*

capacity to enlarge, increase, enhance, and augment the meanings in language can is found in poetry. Here, we see a new horizon of possibilities where new looks at things, and new ways of thinking, can emerge. These possibilities can open new worlds where we can, in Heidegger's word, "dwell" (Heidegger, 1971a, 1971b, 1973). It may be in line with the same perspective that Gadamer (1998) mentioned: that we don't just try to conceive and understand what is in the poem but to reach the kind of world to which the poem belongs or that it projects and displays. In and through poetry, one may say, language can be liberated from the constrictions of ordinary discourse, and new layers of reality can be revealed.

In this sense, it reveals the leap, the shift, and the capacity of the soaring magnitude of expressiveness and the openness of components of discourse, thus allowing everyone to experience this elevation.

In "The Meaning of Meaning," I. A. Richards (1923), in discussing the language of poetry, emphasized the element of being "emotive" versus being "symbolic" as a distinction of the language of poetry. On talking about the distinction of the language of poetry, he did not consider truth or falsehood as the primary determinants of the language of poetry. Rather, he focused on the evocative function as the main fundamental constituent of such language.

> Very much poetry consists of statements, symbolic arrangements capable of truth or falsity but for the sake of the attitudes which their acceptance will evoke. For this purpose, it fortunately happens, or rather it is part of the poet's business to make it happen, that the truth or falsity matters not at all to the acceptance. Provided that the attitude or feeling is evoked, the most important function of such language is fulfilled. Any symbolic function that the words may have is instrumental only and subsidiary to the evocative function. (I. A. Richards, 1923, p. 150)

Swanger (1990) abided by a similar approach and, in "response to poetry," stated that poetry may not consist of a right or wrong language.

While the above analysis of poetry can present one salient of poetry, poetry's language cannot be limited to only evocative function. The evidence in this regard is born from a vast series of poetry in different languages that demonstrate other major functions in addition to the emotive and evocative functions. In Arabic and Persian languages, for example, there are innumerable examples of works of poetry where very deep philosophical or even logical arguments, discussion, viewpoints, and perspectives are presented. Numerous books of philosophy, logic, and metaphysics have been written in strictly explicit poetic language. Among the salient ones, one can refer to Jalaleldin Roumei, Hafis, Sa'adi, Attar, Ghaznavee, Qa'ani, etc.

Film and Poetry 117

Following are some examples to illustrate the point (translations are mine):

So the heart would be as a substance and the world as an accident (formalities).
How can the shadow of the heart serve as the goal for the heart? (Jalaluddin Rummie)
Although my heart made much haste in this desert,
It did not know a single hair but took to hair-splitting.
In my heart shone a thousand suns,
Yet, it never discovered the nature of a single atom completely. Ibn Sina (Avicenna).
Oh, You who bestowed upon wisdom,
All forms of gratitude and appreciation are ultimately yours. (Hadee Sabzevaree)

Eastern ways of thinking have not limited rationality and forms of discourse in some recognized ways of expression but have acknowledged numerous modes of thought associated with numerous forms of discourse to present rationality. The examples mentioned above indicate that poetry can also be used as a language that presents not only evocative and emotive messages but very deep fundamental philosophical points and perspectives. The assumption that poetry enters the scene when the intellect gets feeble needs to be seriously reconsidered. Therefore, the subject matter of poetry can be as vast as possible (to use Leggo's word [1998] "capacious"), covering infinite realms while revealing worlds for dwelling. In the English language, too, one can see, for instance, Immanuel Kant's complex reaction against extreme Cartesian rationalism. Kant discussed the problem of the "sublime," exploring numerous issues in poetic aesthetics. Following Kant, a number of thinkers continued exploring the language of poetry in their works, revealing the application of this discourse as an effective yet inventive way of examining everything.

Johann Gottfried von Herder (1774–1803), enormously inspired by Kant, proposed that the language of poetry is a psychological necessity. His writings and thinking greatly influenced Johann Wolfgang von Goethe (1749–1832), "whose clear perception of linguistic relativism is scattered through his writings. He who doesn't know a foreign language knows nothing of his own" (Freidrich, 1986). These and related ways of thinking also had an influence on leaders of English Romanticism such as Samuel Taylor Coleridge (1772–1832), who studied in Germany and communicated with Wordsworth, Shelley, and other "shapers of what was a fundamentally new world view" (Freidrich, 1986, p. 9).

Almost simultaneous with the formulation of new ideas in questioning the paradigm of language by Frans Boas (1858–1924), Benedetto Croce (1866–1952) propounded a philosophy in which language was considered

118   *Film and Poetry*

the essence of intellectual and emotional values, asserting that language was, to a large extent, poetry.

Along with the same emphasis, we notice the attack on the foundations of linguistic positivism and positivistic semantics by thinkers such as Ludwig Wittgenstein (1899–1951), who revisited the relation of thought, language, and reality.

While introducing the perspective on linguistic relativism and poetic indeterminacy, Freidrich (1986) pinpointed the existence of different worlds within the heart of different languages noting that "it is persons with experience of foreign languages and poetry who feel most acutely that a natural language is a different way not only of talking but of thinking and imagining and of emotional life" (p. 16).

Whether at the individual, sociocultural, or some universal level, language is "inherently, pervasively, and powerfully poetic" (Freidrich, 1986, p. 17). Questioning the distinction between literal and figurative meaning, Gibbs (1995) used ideas and research from psychology, linguistics, philosophy, anthropology, and literary theory and argued that the mind has a poetic structure. His findings overturn the traditional perspective, which holds that thought and language are inherently literal.

Describing the traditional view of the mind as a "mistake," Gibbs (1994) argued that human cognition is fundamentally shaped by various poetic or figurative processes. The traditional view of the mind, he argued, has "imposed limitations on the scholarly study of mental life in cognitive science and the humanities and on everyday folk conceptions of human experience" (Gibbs, 1994). Pinpointing the failure of lexical semantics in its traditional accounts and assumptions, he argued that

> meanings of many polysemous words can be explained in terms of basic metaphors that motivate, among other things, the transfer of English vocabulary from the domain of physical motion and object manipulation and location (e.g., stand in its physical sense) to various social and mental domains (e.g., stand in he took a stand on the matter).
>
> (Gibbs, 1994, p. 223)

In his discussion of poetics, Aristotle referred to all kinds of making in terms of language, both in fiction and poetry. Ricoeur (1991b, p. 449) argues that "through this recovery of the capacity of language to create and re-create, we discover reality itself in the process of being created. So we are connected with this dimension of reality which is unfinished."

Speaking on the role of metaphor and the process of becoming for language, Ricoeur (1991b) described the language of poetry and its significant role: "Language in the making celebrates reality in the making." Making a distinction between the language of ordinary speech and the language of poetry in dealing with reality, he remarkably presented a very striking characteristic of ordinary language versus the language of poetry:

And the rest of our language in ordinary speech and so on has to do with reality as it is already done, as it is finished, as it is there in the sense of the closedness of what is, with its meaning which is already asserted by the consensus of wise people.

(Ricoeur, 1991a, p. 446)

The discourse of poetry is an inventive discourse that cannot and does not need to remain within the confirmation and endorsement of ordinary discourse where relation, imputation, and assertion need to be made in light of some strictly predefined formulations. The language and discourse of poetry recklessly go beyond the borders of considerations and prescriptions. It opens new ways of considerations, new ways of looking, and new ways of thinking.

This is one of the most conspicuous features of the language of poetry: not relying on the existing ways of looking and thinking while introducing new and exquisite ways of reflecting on reality, beings, and things. The discourse of ordinary language needs to have the approval of specific forms of presentation, whereas the discourse of poetic language creates and invents new forms based on the production of new configurations. Therefore, language of poetry does not borrow its underlying components from the prescribed fixed sources of enactment the way the ordinary discourse does. Language of poetry conducts a reflection on a novel and newly sprung modes of thinking while seeking exquisitely artistic and superb relationships among or inside the myriad of realities.

Ricoeur (1991a) discussed the creativity of language in relation to the objective linguistic codes. He claimed that

my philosophical project is to show how human language is inventive despite the objective limits and codes which govern it, to reveal the diversity and potentiality of language which the erosion of the everyday, conditioned by technocratic and political interests, never ceases to obscure. To become aware of the metaphorical and narrative resources of language is to recognize that its flattened or diminished powers can always be rejuvenated to benefit all forms of language usage.

(Ricoeur, 1991b, p. 465)

Examining the meaning of creativity in language and its relationship to the codes, structures, or laws imposed by language, Ricoeur argued that

linguistic creativity constantly strains and stretches the laws and codes of language that regulate it. Roland Barthes described these regulating laws as "fascist" and urged the writer and critic to work at the limits of language, subverting its constraining laws, in order to make way for the free movement of desire, to make language festive. But if the narrative order of language is replete with codes, it is also capable of

120 *Film and Poetry*

creatively violating them. Human creativity is always, in some sense, a response to a regulating order. The imagination is always working on the basis of already established laws. It is its task to make them function creatively, either by originally applying them or by subverting them, or indeed both—what Malraux calls "regulated deformation." There is no function of imagination, no imaginary, that is not structuring or structured, that is not said or about to be said in language. The task of hermeneutics is to charter the unexplored resources of the to-be-said on the basis of the already said. Imagination never resides on the unsaid.

(Ricoeur, 1991b, pp. 470–471)

This philosophical presentation of creativity in language can have significant consequences for film analysis and film therapy since it rigorously suggests that the approach toward a language can develop a difference in the application as well. In other words, one can use the same lexical signs and signifiers of the ordinary language and change them creatively, thus introducing new signifieds on the strength of new signifiers. We may be attuned to our habits of being soaked in the ordinary discourse. Our thoughts can be geared to the lava of ordinary ways of expressivity that we rarely think about being expressive in ways other than the seemingly recognized ways. The point is not to enlarge the magnitude of formalities for saying or extend the latitude for the bombast of saying; the point is the demonstration of the crucial impact of various modes of expressiveness on the thinking and the introduction of new ways of thinking by virtue of new ways of expressiveness. It is in our languages that we construct the reality of ourselves and everything around us. If the language is bound by habitual ways of saying, then the created reality of the language will not be anything except what it ordinarily means to be or what it is allowed to be. But if the language can question the existing parameters and paradigms, it will develop new ways of looking and thinking, albeit new paradigms again. The reality, therefore, is not going to be what it used to be.

The nonordinary language cultivates polysemy and manifests itself in narrative and poetry and poetic narrative. The language here constitutes a world of its own. Mimesis redescribes things while searching for many possibilities. Poetry, in this sense, reaches the essence of things. Contrary to Western ways of thinking, poetry is not just a means for evoking feelings and emotions but can present fundamentally philosophical propositions. There are numerous examples in Eastern philosophy that have been composed in the form of poetry. Also, German romantic folklorists were among the first to propose the concept of the universality of poetry and poetic language, a universality in which they included stories (see, Hairi Yazdi, 1992, for instance).

Some solid arguments and demonstrations indicate that rationality is too significant to be identified with a single technology. Poetry and narratives can be taken into account as embodying distinctive forms of

Film and Poetry 121

language and thought and can demonstrate the reflective forms of discourse. Here language has to be interpreted not only because words are symbols and signs but also because discourse is fundamentally the interpretation of reality. That means that what we utter in one way or the other or what we are subscribed to say defines our realities.

Howl (2015) succinctly demonstrates the power of poetry:

ALLEN GINSBERG: Poetry is a rhythmic articulation of feelings.
ALLEN GINSBERG: I started writing poetry 'cause I fell in love and needed to express my feelings.

Therapists may use films with poetry to promote a sense of artistic and aesthetic connectedness and a higher degree of awareness for both themselves and their clients. They can invite clients to watch poetic films to gain a sense of subtle expressiveness, artistic articulation, and emotional delicacy in response to the world and people. Poetic films may also develop a keen sense of sagacity in viewing the world, a creative predilection in composing and recomposing and decomposing personal stories.

Clients can be invited to see how each poem is a by-product of a creative act, a composition characterized by inventiveness and novelty. Clients can then be asked to bring the same creativity into their lives. Moreover, they can see how poetry brings a shift of attention. Poetry celebrates the possibility of multiple perspectives. The creative emphasis on poetic expressiveness may facilitate helping clients find their own voices and compose their lives mindfully.

The following quote from *Dead Poets Society* (1989) may move in line with the power of poetic inventiveness:

JOHN KEATING: Boys, you must strive to find your own voice. Because the longer you wait to begin, the less likely you are to find it at all. Thoreau said, "Most men lead lives of quiet desperation." Don't be resigned to that. Break out!

Exploring the poetic discourse of creativity in films would help clients see the possibility of their choices. The essence of creativity and critical thinking begins with questioning and challenging the boxes of clinging habits, ordinary and everyday discourses, memory's impact, and the interference of association of ideas.

Creativity challenges the way things are and explores other ways things can be. Creativity fights for otherwise. Creativity targets the unknown, the unfamiliar, and the unexplored.

The creativity of language and creativity of thought unfold and evolve dialectically and yet syllogistically. Creative thought harbors creative language, and creative language nourishes creative thought. The creativity of language defines grammar, grammaticality, and syntax in line with

122 *Film and Poetry*

creating new rules, new openings, and new perspectives. Creative language can give rise to the possibilities of seeing things in a new way. It can augur a change in the interpretations, a revision of the unquestionable, and a challenge of the well-taken-for-granted premises. Creative language can offer a redescription of things, subjects, categories, issues, people, and existence. In the act of creativity being epitomized in an enunciation or articulation, the act of redescription and redefinition parade by virtue of a re-exploration of any compound or composition's consistent constituents.

Poetic spirit may sometimes unfold itself in the content of the film and sometimes emerges in the title of the film.

Splendor in the Grass (1961) is a movie that displays the loss of passionate youthful love and takes its title from Wordsworth's "Ode: Intimations of Mortality."

Enumerating and elucidating examples of forms and contents of poetry in movies may provide clients with a sense of creativity. Therapists may continue to focus on creativity and demonstrate how life can be considered a text that can be recomposed or decomposed based on people's choices.

Elaborating the role of creativity in the poetic discourse and examining its implications in films may help clients see sensible choices in daily activities. The act of creativity is not searching for sameness, is not in pursuit of congruence or compatibility, and is not moving toward convergence. Creativity is not bound to coherence, cohesiveness, conformity, correspondence, or consistency. What is created may not be in coherence or in correspondence with the existing coherence or correspondence, but it can have its own coherence and cohesiveness. Creativity may represent an act of revelation where things are revealed in light of creativity. It can be an act of disclosure where things are cryptically and yet creatively presented. Creatively is not dutifully at the recognized order's service as it is not respectful of the relationships and their establishment. That is why creativity may bring chaos and disorder. However, this chaotic situation is only a result of a comparison between creativity and the previously identified system of order. In other words, the disorder and the unrest of creativity can have their own order if they are examined within their own setting. Creativity is not obedient, but it is cantankerous.

O Brother, Where Art Thou? (2000) is a movie whose opening titles are based on Homer's *The Odyssey.*

The movie depicts the story of three convicts who escape from a chain gang during the Great Depression in Mississippi. They go to retrieve a treasure that one of them (Everett) claims to have buried. They get a lift from a blind man who tells them:

BLIND MAN: I cannot tell you how long this road shall be, but fear not the obstacles in your path, for fate has vouchsafed your reward. Though the road may wind, yea, your hearts grow weary, still, shall ye follow them, even unto your salvation.

Film and Poetry 123

DELMAR O'DONNELL: You work for the railroad, Grampa?

The following quotes from the movie may be examined in terms of diction, tone, and creative implications:

GEORGE NELSON: Cows! I hate cows worse than coppers!
DELMAR O'DONNELL: Oh, George, not the livestock.
ULYSSES EVERETT MCGILL: For him, not for the law. I'm surprised at you, Pete, I gave you credit for more brains than Delmar.
ULYSSES EVERETT MCGILL: A woman is the most fiendish instrument of torture ever devised to bedevil the days of man.

Therapists may use creative interventions and bring poetry into their dialogues with clients while offering hope, faith, and bravery. This may be discussed in reference to films with poetic content. The focus can entail the following discussions and questions:

1　What is it in the poem that brings a subtle tone into self or social awareness?
2　What is in the poem that gives rise to a construction of interpersonal and intrapersonal meaning?
3　How does one apply such construction in one's life?
4　How does the poem selected or the film's poetic content reveal a creative language that can inspire clients to appreciate their own creativity and find their own voice?
5　What are the implications of the creative voice and its power to enrich meanings in life?
6　How does the poem's scope and breadth in the film or the poetic content of the film serve as a source of inspiration?
7　How does one live poetically in the world?
8　How does one create and invent one's poetic expressiveness that can have an impact on one's way of living?
9　Having understood the power of poetic expressiveness in creating new realities and new perspectives, how does one apply that language to beat anxiety, fear, and depression?
10　How can the power of creativity and poetic expressiveness teach clients to reflect on making positive changes in their lives?
11　How can poetic pieces in a film such as *The Sound of Music* (1965) serve as a source of inspiration, hope, and emotional management?
12　What are the implications of a poetic language for mindfulness?
13　Can poetry give rise to mindfulness?
14　What is the role of films in promoting and cultivating both poetic spirit and mindfulness?

Bibliography

Abu-Rabi, I. M. (1996). *Intellectual origins of Islamic resurgence in the modern Arab world*. Albany State University.

Albee, G. W. (1981). Politics, power, prevention, and social change. In J. M. Joffee & G. W. Albee (Eds.), *Prevention through political action and social change* (pp. 5–25). University Press of New England.

Arthur, A. Z. (1966). A decision-making approach to psychological assessment in the clinic. *Journal of Consulting Psychology*, 30, 433–438.

Alexander, M. (1995). Cinemeducation: An innovative approach to teaching multi-cultural diversity in medicine. *Annals of Behavioral Sciences and Medical Education*, 2(1), 23–28.

Alexander, M., Hall, M., & Pettice, Y. (1994). Cinemeducation: An innovative approach to teaching psychosocial medical care. *Family Medicine*, 26, 430–433.

Alexander, M., & Waxman, D. (2000). Cinemeducation: Teaching family systems through the movies. *Families, Systems, & Health*, 18(4), 455–466.

Anderson, L.F. (1979). *Schooling and citizenship in a global age: an exploration of the meaning and significance of global education*. Social Studies Development Center.

Andreski, S. (1972). *Social sciences and sorcery*. Deutsch.

Austen, J. (1991). *Pride and prejudice*. Knopf.

Austin, J. L. (1962). *How to do things with words*. Oxford University Press.

Austin, T. (1994). *Poetic voices. Discourse linguistics and the poetic text*. The University of Alabama Press.

Austin, J. H. (1999). *Zen and the brain: Toward an understanding of meditation and consciousness*. MIT Press.

Baars, B. J. (1997). *In the theatre of consciousness*. Oxford University Press.

Bakan, D. (1966). *The duality of human existence*. Beacon Press.

Bakan, D. (1967). Idolatry in religion and science. In D. Bakan (Ed.), *On method: Toward a reconstruction of psychological investigation* (pp. 150–159). Jossey-Bass. (Original work published 1961)

Bakan, D. (1996). The crisis in psychology. *Journal of Social Distress and the Homeless*, 5(4), 335–342.

Baltes, P. B., & Smith, J. (1987, August). *Toward a psychology of wisdom and its ontogenesis*. Paper presented at the Ninety-Fifth Annual Convention of the American Psychological Association, New York.

Bibliography   125

Baltes, P. B., & Smith, J. (1990). Toward a psychology of wisdom and its onto-genesis. In R. J. Sternberg (Ed.), *Wisdom: Its nature, origins, and development* (pp. 87–120). Cambridge University Press.

Baltes, P. B., Glück, J., & Kunzmann, U. (2002). *Wisdom: Its structure and function in regulating successful lifespan development.* In C. R. Snyder & S. J. Lopez (Eds.), *The handbook of positive psychology* (pp. 327–347). Oxford University Press.

Baltes, P. B., & Staudinger, U. M. (2000). Wisdom: A metaheuristic (pragmatic) to orchestrate mind and virtue toward excellence. *American Psychologist, 55*, 122–136.

Barrow, R., & Woods, R. (2006). *An introduction to philosophy of education* (Rev. 4th ed.). Routledge.

Bellah, R., Madsen, R., Sullivan, W. M., Swidler, A. & Tipton, S. M. (1991). *The good society.* Alfred A. Knopf.

Bercherie, P. (2005). *Lacan.* L'Harmattan.

Berg, B. L. (2009). *Qualitative research methods for the social sciences.* Pearson.

Berg-Cross, L., Jennings, P., & Baruch, R. (1990). Cinematherapy: Theory and application. *Psychotherapy in Private Practice*, 8(1), 135–156. doi:10.1300/ J294v08n01_15.

Bernal, J. D. (1939). *The social function of science.* Routledge.

Bhatia, S. (2002). Orientalism in Euro-American and Indian psychology: Historical representations of "natives" in colonial and postcolonial contexts. *History of Psychology*, 5, 376–398.

Bierman, J., Krieger, A., & Leifer, M. (2003). Group cinematherapy as a treatment modality for adolescent girls. *Residential Treatment for Children & Youth*, 21(1), 1–15. https://doi.org/10.1300/j007v21n01_01.

Brigham, C. C. (1923). *A study of American intelligence.* Princeton University Press.

Broca, P. (1864). *On the phenomena of hybridity in the genus homo.* Longman, Green, Longman, & Roberts.

Bronowski, J. (1956). *Science and human values.* Penguin.

Bruner, J. (1986). *Actual minds possible worlds.* Harvard University Press.

Bruner, J. (1990). *Acts of meaning.* Harvard University Press.

Bruner, J. (1991). The narrative construction of reality. *Critical Inquiry*, 18, 1–21.

Bruner, J. (2006). *The selected works of Jerome Bruner* (Vol. 2). Routledge.

Bryant, C. G. A. (1985). *Positivism in social theory and research.* Macmillan.

Carrol, N. (1988). Film/mind analogies: The case of Hugo Munsterberg. *The Journal of Aesthetics and Art Criticism, 46(4)*, 489–500. doi:10.1111/1540_6245. jaac46.4.0489.

Case, R. (1993). *Key elements of a global perspective. Social Education*, 57, 318-325.

Chomsky, N. (Ed.). (1996). *The humanities in the USA during the cold war.* Simon & Schuster.

Clark, K. B. (1965). *Dark ghetto: Dilemmas of social power.* Harper Torch Books.

Code, H. (1995). How do we know? Questions of method in feminist practice. In S. Burt & L. Code (Eds.), *Changing methods: Feminists transforming practice* (pp. 13–43). Broadview Press.

Coombs, J. (1989). *Towards a defensible conception of a global perspective.* Research and Development in Global Studies, University of British Columbia.

126 *Bibliography*

Crum, A. J., & Lyddy, C. (2014). De-stressing stress: The power of mindsets and the art of stressing mindfully. In A. Ie, C. T. Ngnoumen, & E. J. Langer (Eds.), *The Wiley Blackwell handbook of mindfulness*. Wiley-Blackwell.

Csikszentmihalyi, M. (1990). *Flow: The psychology of optimal experience*. Harper-Collins.

Cushman, P. (1990). Why the self is empty. Toward a historically situated psychology. *American Psychologist*, 45, 599–611. doi:10.1037/0003-066X.45.5.599.

Dale, G., & Wrisberg, C. (1996). The use of a performance profiling technique in a team setting: Getting the athletes and coach on the "same page." *The Sport Psychologist*, 10(3), 261–277. doi:10.1123/tsp.10.3.261.

Danziger, K. (1990). *Constructing the subject: Historical origins of psychological research*. Cambridge University Press.

Davidson, J. (2000). Social anxiety disorder under scrutiny. *Depression and Anxiety*, 11(3), 93–98. doi:10.1002/(sici)1520-6394(2000)11:3<93::aid-da2>3.0.co;2-7.

De Jachger, H., Di Paolo, E., & Gallagher, S. (2010). Can social interaction constitute social cognition? *Trends in Cognitive Sciences*, 14, 441–447.

Delby, R. G. A. (1996). *Uncertain knowledge*. Cambridge University Press.

Demir, M., Ozen, A., Dogan, A., Bilyk, N. A., & Tyrell, F. A. (2011). I matter to my friend, there I am happy: Friendship, mattering, and happiness. *Journal of Happiness Studies*, 12, 983–1005.

Dermer, S., & Hutchings, J. (2000). Utilizing movies in family therapy: Applications for individuals, couples, and families. *The American Journal of Family Therapy*, 28(2), 163–180. doi:10.1080/019261800261734.

Derrida, J. (1976). *Of grammatology*. Johns Hopkins University Press.

De Saussure, F. (1966). *Course in general linguistics*. McGraw-Hill.

DeWall, C. N., Baumeister, R. F., Mead, N. L., & Vohs, K. D. (2011). How leaders self-regulate their task performance: Evidence that power promotes diligence, depletion, and disdain. *Journal of Personality and Social Psychology*, 100(1), 47–65.

Diamond, D. (2016). The Red Shoes: A fairy tale within a ballet within a film. *Psychoanalytic Psychology*, 33(Suppl. 1), S104–S119. doi:10.1037/pap0000071.

DiBerardinis, J. D., Barwind, J., Flanninam, R. R., & Jenkins, V. (1983). Enhanced interpersonal relation as predictor of athletic performance. *International Journal of Sport Psychology*, 14, 243–251.

Dick, B. (2002). *Anatomy of film* (4th ed.). Bedford/St. Martin's.

Diener, E. (Ed.). (2009). *The science of well-being: The collected works of Ed Diener*. Springer.

Diener, E., Lucas, R., & Scollon, C. (2006). Beyond the hedonic treadmill: Revising the adaptation theory of wellbeing. *American Psychologist*, 61, 305–314.

Diener, E., Tay, L., & Myers, D. G. (2011). The religion paradox: If religion makes people happy, why are so many dropping out? *Journal of Personality and Social Psychology*, 101(6), 1278–1290.

Dittmann-Kohli, F., & Baltes, P. B. (1990). Toward a neo-functionalist conception of adult development: Wisdom as a prototypical case of intellectual growth. In C. Alexander & E. Langer (Eds.), *Higher stages of human development* (pp. 53–78). Oxford University Press.

Durgnat, R. (1982). Review: *Psychoanalysis and cinema* by Christian Metz. *Film Quarterly*, 36(2), 58–64. doi:10.2307/3696998.

Eco, U. (1976). *A theory of semiotics*. Indiana University Press.

Bibliography 127

Epley, N., Savitsky, K., & Gilovich, T. (2002). Empathy neglect: Reconciling the spotlight effect and the correspondence bias. *Journal of Personality and Social Psychology*, 83(2), 300–312. doi:10.1037/0022-3514.83.2.300.

Fatemi, S. M. (2008). Questioning the mastery of signs/celebrating the mystery of symbols. *Educational Insights*, 12(1), 1–17.

Fatemi, S. M. (2014). From Kierkegaard to Langer (From Kierkegaard's paradox to Langer's psychology of possibility). *Frontiers in Psychology*. doi:10.3389/fpsyg.2014.01161.

Fatemi, S. M. (2016a). *Critical mindfulness: Exploring Langerian models.* Springer.

Fatemi, S. M. (2016b). Langerian mindfulness and liminal performing spaces. In A. L. Baltzell (Ed.), *Mindfulness and performance (Current perspectives in social and behavioral sciences)* (pp. 112–124). Cambridge University Press.

Fatemi, S. M. (2016c). Mindfulness and perceived control: Controlling the impossibility of controllability. In J. W. Reich & F. J. Infurna (Eds.), *Perceived control: Theory, research, and practice in the first 50 years* (pp. 131–146). Oxford University Press.

Fatemi, S. M. (2018a). *Phenomenological psychology of mindfulness: Psychology of presence.* Lexington.

Fatemi, S. M. (2018b). *The psychological power of language.* Routledge.

Fatemi, S. M., & Langer, E. J. (2018). Langerian mindfulness and its psychotherapeutic implications: Recomposing/decomposing mindlessly constructed life stories. In B. Kirkcaldy (Ed.), *Psychotherapy, literature and the visual and performing arts* (pp. 43–53). Palgrave Macmillan.

Fatemi, S. M., Ward, E. D., & Langer, E. J. (2016). Peak performance: Langerian mindfulness and flow. In A. L. Baltzell (Ed.), *Mindfulness and performance (Current perspectives in social and behavioral sciences)* (pp. 101–111). Cambridge University Press.

Faure, G. O. (2000). Negotiations to set up joint ventures in China. *International Negotiation*, 5(1), 157–189.

Feigl, H. (1969). The origin and spirit of logical positivism. In P. Achinstein & S. F. Baker (Eds.), *The legacy of logical positivism* (pp. 3–24). Johns Hopkins Press.

Fine, M. (1992). *Disruptive voices: The possibilities of feminist research.* University of Michigan Press.

Fine, M. (1994). Dis-stance and other stances: Negotiations of power inside feminist research. In A. Gitlin (Ed.), *Power and method: Political activism and educational research* (pp. 13–35). Routledge.

Fredrickson, B. L., & Losada, M. F. (2005). Positive Affect and the Complex Dynamics of Human Flourishing. *American Psychologist*, 60(7), 678–686. https://doi.org/10.1037/0003-066X.60.7.678

Freire, P. (1972a). *Pedagogy of the oppressed.* Penguin.

Freire, P. (1998a). *Pedagogy of freedom: Ethics, democracy, and civic courage.* Rowman and Littlefield. Freire, P. (1972a). Pedagogy of the oppressed. Penguin.

Fine, M. (2002). Carolyn Sherif award address: The presence of an absence. *Psychology of Women Quarterly*, 26, 9–24.

Fleming, M., Piedmont, R., & Hiam, C. (1990). Images of madness: Feature films in teaching psychology. *Teaching of Psychology*, 17(3), 185–187.

Freire, P. (2000). *Pedagogy of the heart.* Continuum Press.

Freud, S., & Brill, A. (2015). *Studies in hysteria.* Nabu Press.

128 *Bibliography*

Frey-Rohn, L., Engreen, F. E., & Engreen, E. K. (1974). *From Freud to Jung: A comparative study of the psychology of the unconscious.* Putnam.

Friedrich, P. (1986). *The language parallax.* University of Texas Press.

Gabbard, G., & Gabbard, K. (1999). *Psychiatry and the cinema.* American Psychiatric Press.

Gadamer, H. G. (1988). *Truth and method.* Crossroad.

Gergen, K. J. (1990). Towards a postmodern psychology. *Humanistic Psychologist,* 18(1), 23–34.

Gergen, K. (1991). *The saturated self.* Basic Books.

Gibbs, R. W. (1995). *The poetics of mind.* Cambridge University Press.

Gills, B. R. (2002). *Democratizing globalization and globalizing democracy.* Annals of the American Academy of Political and Social Science, Vol. 581, Globalization and Democracy pp. 158–171.

Ginges, J., Atran, S., Sachdeva, A., & Medin, D. (2011). Psychology out of the laboratory: The challenge of violent extremism. *American Psychologist, 66,* 507–519.

Goleman, D. (2003). *Destructive emotions: How can we overcome them? A scientific dialogue with the Dalai Lama.* Bantam Dell.

Gottman, J. M. (1994). *What predicts divorce? The relationship between marital processes and marital outcomes.* Lawrence Erlbaum Associates, Inc.

Gould, S. J. (1996). *The mismeasure of man* (Revised and expanded ed.). Norton.

Grosse, P. (1997). Psychologische menschenführung und die deutsche kolonialpolitik, 1900–1940 [Psychological guidance and German colonial politics, 1900–1940]. In P. Mecheril & T. Teo (Eds.), *Psychologie und rassismus [Psychology and racism]* (pp. 19–41). Rowohlt.

Grove, W. M., Zald, D. H., Lebow, B. S., Snitz, B. E., & Nelson, C. (2000). Clinical versus mechanical prediction: A meta-analysis. *Psychological Assessment,* 12, 19–30.

Guba, E. G., & Lincoln, Y. S. (1989). *Fourth generation evaluation.* Sage.

Guba, E. G., & Lincoln, Y. S. (1994). Competing paradigms in qualitative research. In N. K. Denzin & Y. S. Lincoln (Eds.), *Handbook of qualitative research* (pp. 105–117). Sage.

Habermas, J. (1972). *Knowledge and human interests* (J. J. Shapiro, Trans.). Beacon Press. (Original work published 1968)

Habermas, J. (1973a). *Communication and the evolution of society.* Beacon Press.

Habermas, J. (1973b). *Legitimation crisis.* Beacon Press.

Habermas, J. (1975). *Legitimation crisis.* Beacon Press. (Original work published 1973)

Habermas, J. (1979). *Communication and the evolution of society.* Heinemann.

Ha'iri Yazdi, M. (1992). *The principles of epistemology in Islamic philosophy.* State University of New York Press.

Hakimi, M. R. (1997). *Ejtehad Va Taghleed darfalsafe [Ejtehad or imitation in philosophy].* Daeele Ma.

Hakimi, M.R. (2002). Payame Javedaneh. Dalile-Ma.

Hakimi, M. R. (2004). *Elaheeyate Elahee va elaheeyate basharee [Islamic theology and man driven theology].* Daleele Ma Publications.

Hakimi, M. R. (2013). *Ejtehad va taqleed dar falsafe [Ijtihad and mimicry in philosophy].* Daleele Ma.

Hakimi, M. R., Hakimi, A., & Hakimi, M. (2005). *Alhayat [Life].* Daleele Ma.

Hakimi, M. R., Hakimi, A., & Hakimi, M. (2007). *Alhayat [Life].* Daleele Ma.

Hakimi, M. R., Hakimi, A., & Hakimi, M. (2011). *Alhayat [Life].* Daleele Ma.

Bibliography   129

Hall, J. H., & Fincham, F. D. (2005). Self-forgiveness: The stepchild of forgiveness research. *Journal of Social and Clinical Psychology*, 24(5), 621–637.

Hammond, K. R., Hursch, C. J., & Todd, F. J. (1964). Analyzing the components of clinical influence. *Psychological Review*, 71, 438–456.

Hanvey, R. (1976). *An attainable global perspective*. Center for Teaching International Relations.

Hare, R., & Secord, P. F. (1972). *The explanation of social behavior*. Basil Blackwell.

Harrani, H. E. S. (1984). *TohafolOqool anAle Rasool (Salavatollahalayh)*. Darol Eyha Atorath Alarabi.

Heidegger, M. (1953). *Being and time*. State University of New York Press.

Heiddeger, M. (1971a). *Language, thought and poetry* (A. Hofstadter, Trans.). Harper and Row.

Heiddeger, M. (1971b). *On the way to language*. Harper & Row.

Heidegger, M. (1973). Art and space. *Man and World*, 6, 3–8.

Heidegger, M. (1995). *The fundamental concepts of metaphysics: World, finitude, solitude*. Indiana University Press.

Heidegger, M. (1999). *Contributions to philosophy*. Indiana University Press.

Herda, E. A. (1999). *Research conversations and narrative. A critical hermeneutic orientation in participatory inquiry*. Praeger.

Hesley, J. W., & Hesley, J. G. (1998). *Rent two films and let's talk in the morning: Using popular movies in psychotherapy*. Wiley.

Hessen, B. (1971). *The social and economic roots of Newton's principia*. Howard Fertig.

Holton, G. (1993). *Science and anti-science*. Harvard University Press.

Holzkamp, K. (1991). Experience of self and scientific objectivity. In C. W. Tolman & W. Maiers (Eds.), *Critical psychology: Contributions to an historical science of the subject* (pp. 65–80). Cambridge University Press.

Horkheimer, M. (1992). Traditional and critical theory. In D. Ingram & J. Simon Ingram (Eds.), *Critical theory: The essential readings* (pp. 239–254). Paragon House. (Original work published 1937)

Houtman, G. (2006). Double or quits. *Anthropology Today*, 22(6), 1–3.

Jafari, M. T. (1995). *Mathnavi Ma'navi: A critical interpretation* (Vol. 4). Alame Jafari Publications.

Jafari, M. T. (2004). *Dar Mahzare Hakim [In the presence of wisdom]*. Alame Jafari Publications.

Jafari, M.T. (2006). *Tarjomeh va tafseere nahjolbalaghe*. Daftare Nashre Farhange Islamee

James, W. (2002). *The varieties of religious experience*. Modern Library.

Jänicke, S., Franzini, G., Cheema, M., & Scheuermann, G. (2016). Visual text analysis in digital humanities. *Computer Graphics Forum*, 36(6), 226–250. doi:10.1111/cgf.12873.

Janicke, S. H., & Oliver, M. B. (2017). The relationship between elevation, connectedness, and compassionate love in meaningful films. *Psychology of Popular Media Culture*, 6(3), 274–289. https://doi.org/10.1037/ppm0000105

Janicke, S., & Ramasubramanian, S. (2017). Spiritual media experiences, trait transcendence, and enjoyment of popular films. *Journal of Media and Religion*, 16(2), 51–66. doi:10.1080/15348423.2017.1311122.

Jaspers, K. (1997). *General psychopathology* (J. Hoenig & M. W. Hamilton, Trans.). Johns Hopkins University Press.

130 *Bibliography*

Johnston, J. (2001). *The American body in context, an anthology.* SR Books.

Jung, C. G. (1953). *Collected works. Vol. 12. Psychology and alchemy.* Pantheon Books.

Jung, C. G. (1961). *Memories, dreams, reflections.* Pantheon.

Jung, C. G. (1966a). *Collected works: Vol. 16.* The practice of psychotherapy: *Essays on the psychology of the transference and other subjects.* Princeton University Press.

Jung, C. G. (1966b). *Collected works: Vol. 7.* Two essays on analytical psychology (Rev. 2nd ed.). Routledge.

Jung, C. G. (1967). *Collected works: Vol. 17.* The development of personality Princeton University Press.

Jung, C. G. (1968). *Analytical psychology: Its theory and practise.* Princeton University Press.

Jung, C. G. (1970a). *Four archetypes; mother, rebirth, spirit, trickster.* Princeton University Press.

Jung, C. G. (1970b). *Collected works: Vol. 14. Mysterium coniunctionis* (2nd ed.). Routledge.

Jung, C. G. (1971). *Psychological types: The collected works* (Vol. 6.). Routledge and Kegan Paul.

Jung, C. G. (1973). Synchronicity: An acausal connecting principle (2nd ed.). Princeton University Press.

Jung, C. G. (1974a). *Dreams.* Princeton University Press.

Jung, C. G. (1974b). The Freud/Jung letters: The correspondence between Sigmund Freud and C. G. Jung (W. McGuire, Ed., & R. F. C. Hull and R. Mannheim, Trans.). Princeton University Press (Original work published 1917)

Jung, C. G., von Franz, M. L., Henderson, J. L., Jacobi, J., & Jaffé, A. (1964). *Man and his symbols.* Doubleday.

Kabat-Zinn, J. (1994). *Wherever you go, there you are: Mindfulness meditation in everyday life.* Hyperion

Kabat-Zinn, J. (2003a). Mindfulness-based interventions in context: Past, present, and future. *Clinical Psychology: Science and Practice,* 10(2), 144–156.

Kabat-Zinn, J. (2003b). Mindfulness-based stress reduction (MBSR). *Constructivism in the Human Sciences,* 8(2), 73–83.

Kabat-Zinn, J. (2005). *Coming to our senses: Healing ourselves and the world through mindfulness.* Hyperion.

Kahneman, D., & Frederick, S. (2002). *Representativeness revisited: Attribute substitution in intuitive judgment.* In T. Gilovich, D. Griffin, & D. Kahneman (Eds.), *Heuristics and biases: The psychology of intuitive judgment* (pp. 49–81). Cambridge University Press. doi:10.1017/CBO9780511808098.004.

Karlinsky, H. (2003). *Doc Hollywood* north: Part I. The educational applications of movies in psychiatry. *CPA Bulletin,* 35, 9–12.

Katz, C. (1992). All the world is staged: Intellectuals and the projects of ethnography. *Environment and Planning D: Society and Space,* 10, 495–510.

Kelman, H. C. (1965). *International behavior: A social–psychological analysis.* Holt, Rinehart, & Winston.

Kierkegaard, S. (1992). *Concluding unscientific postscript* (H. V. Hong & E. H. Hong, Trans.). Princeton University Press. (Original work published 1846)

Kremenyuk, V. A. (Ed.). (2002). *International negotiation: Analysis, approaches, issues.* Jossey-Bass.

Bibliography 131

Kruglanski, A. W., & Orehek, E. (2007). Partitioning the domain of social influence: Dual mode and system models and their alternatives. *Annual Review of Psychology*, 58, 291–316.

Kuhn, T. (1970). *The structure of scientific revolutions* (2nd ed.). University of Chicago Press.

Lacan, J. (1994). *The four fundamental concepts of psychoanalysis* (J. A. Miller, Ed., & A. Sheridan, Trans.). Penguin.

Lampropoulos, G. K., Kazantzis, N., & Deane, F. P. (2004). Psychologists' use of motion pictures in clinical practice. *Professional Psychology: Research and Practice*, 35(5), 535–541.

Landesman, C. (1997). *An introduction to epistemology.* Blackwell Science.

Langer, E. J. (1975). The illusion of control. *Journal of Personality and Social Psychology*, 32, 311–328.

Langer, E. J. (1989). *Mindfulness.* Addison-Wesley.

Langer, E. J. (1997). *The power of mindful learning.* Addison-Wesley.

Langer, E. J. (2000). Mindful learning. *Current Directions in Psychological Science*, 9, 220–223.

Langer, E. J. (2002). Well-being: Mindfulness versus positive evaluation. In C. R. Snyder & S. J. Lopez (Eds.), *Handbook of positive psychology* (pp. 214–230). New York: Oxford University Press.

Langer, E. J. (2005). *On becoming an artist: Reinventing yourself through mindful creativity.* Ballantine Books.

Langer, E. J. (2009). *Counterclockwise: Mindful health and the power of possibility.* Ballantine Books.

Langer, E. J., & Abelson, R. P. (1974). A patient by any other name: Clinician group difference in labeling bias. *Journal of Consulting and Clinical Psychology*, 42, 4–9. doi:10.1037/h0036054.

Langer, E. J., Bashner, R., & Chanowitz, B. (1985). Decreasing prejudice by increasing discrimination. *Journal of Personality and Social Psychology*, 49, 113–120. doi:10.1037/0022-3514.49.1.113.

Langer, E. J., Blank, A., & Chanowitz, B. (1978). The mindlessness of ostensibly thoughtful action: The role of "placebic" information in interpersonal interaction. *Journal of Personality and Social Psychology*, 36(6), 635–642. doi:10.1037/00223514.36.6.635.

Langer, E. J., & Rodin, J. (1976). The effects of choice and enhanced personal responsibility for the aged: A field experiment. *Journal of Personality and Social Psychology*, 34(2), 191–198.

Lanyon, R. I. (1972). Technological approach to the improvement of decision making in mental health services. *Journal of Consulting and Clinical Psychology*, 39, 43–48.

Lasn, K. (1999). *Culture jam, the uncooling of America.* Eagle Brook.

Lather, P. (1991). *Getting smart: Feminist research and pedagogy with/in the postmodern.* Routledge.

Latour, B. (2004). How to talk about the body? The normative dimension of science studies. *Body and Society*, 10, 205–229. doi:10.1177/1357034X04042943.

Lausic, D., Tennebaum, G., Eccles, D., Jeong, A., & Johnson, T. (2009). Intrateam communication and performance in double tennis. *Research Quarterly for Exercise and Sport*, 80, 281–290.

132   Bibliography

Leggo, C. (1999). *Teaching to wonder, responding to poetry in the secondary classroom*. Pacific Educational Press.

Leggo, C. (1999a). *Tangled lines* [Unpublished manuscript].

Leggo, C. (1999b). *Teaching to wonder, responding to poetry in the secondary classroom*. Pacific Educational Press.

Levy, B., & Langer, E. (1994). Aging free from negative stereotypes: Successful memory in China and among the American deaf. *Journal of Personality and Social Psychology, 66*, 989–997.

Lipton, B. (2005). *The biology of belief: Unleashing the power of consciousness, matter, and miracles*. Mountain of Love/Elite Books.

Lotringer, S. (Ed.). (1996). *Foucault live: Michael Foucault: Collected interviews, 1961–1984* (L. Hochroth & J. Johnson, Trans.). Semiotext(e).

Lyotard, J.-F. (1984). *The postmodern condition: A report on knowledge* (G. Bennington & B. Massumi, Trans.). University of Minnesota Press. (Original work published 1979)

Maher, M. (1999). Relationship-based change: A feminist qualitative research case. In M. Kopala & L. A. Suzuki (Eds.), *Using qualitative methods in psychology* (pp. 187–198). Sage.

Malcolm, W. M., & Greenberg, L. S. (2000). Forgiveness as a process of change in individual psychotherapy. In M. E. McCullough, K. I. Pargament, & C. E. Thoresen (Eds.), *Forgiveness: Theory, research, and practice* (pp. 179–202). Guilford.

Marsick, E. (2010). Cinematherapy with preadolescents experiencing parental divorce: A collective case study. *The Arts in Psychotherapy, 37*(4), 311–318. https://doi.org/10.1016/j.aip.2010.05.006

McCullough, L., & Osborn, K. (2004). Short term dynamic psychotherapy goes to Hollywood: The treatment of performance anxiety in cinema. *Journal of Clinical Psychology, 60*(8), 841–852. doi:10.1002/jclp.20042.

McLellan, B. (1999). The prostitution of psychotherapy: A feminist critique. *British Journal of Guidance and Counseling, 27*, 325–337.

Meadowcroft, J. M., & Reeves, B. (1989). Influence of story schema development on children's attention to television. *Communication Research, 16*(3), 352–374. doi:10.1177/009365089016003003.

Merryfield, M. M. (1997). A framework for teacher education in global perspectives. In M. M. Merryfield, E. Jarchow, & S. Pickert (Eds.), *Preparing teachers to teach global perspectives: A handbook for teacher education* (pp. 1–24). Corwin Press.

Merryfield, M. M. (2009). Moving the center of global education: From imperial world views that divide the world to double consciousness, contrapuntal pedagogy, hybridity, and cross-cultural competence. In J. L. Tucker (Eds.), *Visions in global education. The globalization of curriculum and pedagogy in teacher education and schools: Perspectives from Canada, Russia, and the United States* (pp. 219–223). Peter Lang.

Metz, C. (1974). *The imaginary signifier. Psychoanalysis and the cinema*. Indiana University Press.

Metz, C. (2000). *The imaginary signifier*. Indiana University Press.

Metz, C., & Britton, C. (1982). *The imaginary signifier*. Indiana University Press.

Miles, S. (1998) Consumerism as a way of life. Sage Publications Ltd. http://dx.doi.org/10.4135/9781446217115

Bibliography   133

Minh-Ha, T. T. (1986–1987). Difference: A special third world women issue. In T. T. Minh-Ha (Ed.), *She, the inappropriate/d other, Discourse 8*.

Minh-Ha, T. T. (1989). *Woman, native, other: Writing postcoloniality and feminism*. Indiana University Press.

Morgan, B. (2002). Critical practice in community-based ESL programs: A Canadian perspective. *Journal of Language, Identity, and Education*, 1(2), 141–162.

Mulvey, L. (1976). Visual pleasure and narrative cinema. In B. Nichols (Ed.), *Movies and methods* (Vol. 1, pp. 305–315). California University Press.

Mulvey, L. (1993). Some thoughts on theories of fetishism in the context of contemporary culture. *October*, 65, 3–20.

Mulvey, L., & Wollen, P. (1976). A written discussion. *Afterimage*, 6, 31–39.

Münsterberg, H. (1970). *The film: A psychological study*. Dover.

Nader, L. (Ed.). (1996). *Naked science: Anthropological inquiry into boundaries, power and knowledge*. Routledge.

Nader, L. (2000). *Naked science*. Pergamon.

Nasr, S. H. (Ed.). (2007). *The essential Seyed Hossein Nasr*. World Wisdom.

Nelson, E. (2002). Using film to teach psychology: A resource of film study guides. Retrieved from http://teachpsych.org/otrp/resources/nelson06.pdf.

Nelson, G., & Prilleltensky, I. (2005). *Community psychology: In pursuit of liberation and wellbeing*. Palgrave Macmillan.

Niemiec, R. M. (2005). Friendship: A spiritual antidote to loneliness [Review of the film *The station agent*]. *PsycCRITIQUES – Contemporary Psychology: APA Review of Books*, 50(24), Article15. doi:10.1037/041054.

Niemiec, R. M. (2007). What is a positive psychology film? [Review of the film *The pursuit of happyness*]. *PsycCRITIQUES – Contemporary Psychology: APA Review of Books*, 52(38), Article18. doi:10.1037/a0008960.

Niemiec, R. M. (2008a). A call to the sacred [Review of the film *The flight of the red balloon*]. *PsycCRITIQUES – Contemporary Psychology: APA Review of Books*, 53(48). doi:10.1037/a0014313.

Niemiec, R. M. (2008b). The visitor: The positive snowball effect. *Positive Psychology News Daily*. http://positivepsychologynews.com/news/ryan-niemiec/200812251390.

Niemiec, R. M. (2010a). The true meaning of character [Review of the film *Invictus*]. *PsycCRITIQUES – Contemporary Psychology: APA Review of Books*, 55 (19), Article9. doi:10.1037/a0019539.

Niemiec, R. M. (2010b). A wonderland journey through positive psychology interventions [Review of the film *Alice in wonderland*]. *PsycCRITIQUES – Contemporary Psychology: APA Review of Books*, 55(31), Article9. doi:10.1037/90014313.

Niemiec, R. M. (2011). Positive psychology cinemeducation: A review of *Happy. International Journal of Wellbeing*, 1(3), 326–332.

Niemiec, R. M. (2012a). The best possible self exercise (boosts hope). Psych Central. http://blogs.psychcentral.com/character-strengths/2012/09/the-best-possible-self-exercise-boosts-hope/.

Niemiec, R. M. (2012b). Cinematic elevation and cinematic admiration: Can watching movies positively impact you?Amplifier – American Psychological Association Division 46. http://www.apa.org/divisions/div46/Amplifier_Summer2012.pdf.

Niemiec, R. M. (2012c). Mindful living: Character strengths interventions as pathways for the five mindfulness trainings. *International Journal of Wellbeing*, 2 (1), 22–33.

134 Bibliography

Niemiec, R. M. (2013). VIA character strengths: Research and practice (The first 10 years). In H. H. Knoop & A. Delle Fave (Eds.), *Well-being and cultures: Perspectives on positive psychology* (pp. 11–30). Springer.

Niemiec, R. M. (2014). *Mindfulness and character strengths*. Hogrefe.

Niemiec, R. M., & Clyman, J. (2009). Temperance: The quiet virtue finds a home [Review of movie *Twilight*]. *PsycCRITIQUES – Contemporary Psychology: APA Review of Books*, 54(46). doi:10.1037/a0017924.

Niemiec, R. M., & Ferland, D. (2006). The layers of transformation. [Review of film Batman Begins]. *PsycCRITIQUES – Contemporary Psychology: APA Review of Books*, 51(2), Article20. doi:10.1037/05206611.

Niemiec, R. M., & Oatley, K. (2011). *On film and flourishing* [Unpublished manuscript].

Niemiec, R. M., Rashid, T., & Spinella, M. (2012). Strong mindfulness: Integrating mindfulness and character strengths. *Journal of Mental Health Counseling*, 34 (3), 240–253.

Niemiec, R. M., & Schulenberg, S. E. (2011). Understanding death attitudes. The integration of movies, positive psychology, and meaning management. *Death Studies*, 35(5), 387–407.

Niemiec, R. M., & Wedding, D. (2006). The role of the psychotherapist in movies. *Advances in Medical Psychotherapy and Psychodiagnosis*, 12, 73–83.

Noorani, A. (1980). *Talkheesol Mohassal, known as Naqde Mohassal*. University of Tehran, McGill.

Oatley, K. (2007). Coming together. [Review of the film *Away From Her*]. *PsycCRITIQUES – Contemporary Psychology: APA Review of Books*, 52(39), Article18. doi:10.1037/90009137.

Oatley, K. (2011). *Such stuff as dreams: The psychology of fiction*. Wiley-Blackwell.

Oatley, K. (2012). Faith [Review of film *Salmon Fishing in the Yemen*]. *PsycCRITIQUES – Contemporary Psychology: APA Review of Books*, 57(34). doi:10.1037/a0029780.

Oatley, K., & Djikic, M. (2018). Psychology of narrative art. *Review of General Psychology*, 22(2), 161–168. doi:10.1037/gpr0000113.

Oatley, K., Dunbar, R., & Budelmann, F. (2018). Imagining possible worlds. *Review of General Psychology*, 22(2), 121–124. doi:10.1037/gpr0000149.

Oliner, S. P. (2005). Altruism, forgiveness, empathy, and intergroup apology. *Humboldt Journal of Social Relations*, 29, 8–39.

Oliver, M. B., & Bartch, A. (2010). Appreciation as audience response: Exploring entertainment gratifications beyond hedonism. *Human Communication Research*, 36, 53–81.

Oman, D. (2011). Compassionate love: Accomplishments and challenges in an emerging scientific/spiritual research field. *Mental Health, Religion & Culture*, 14 (9), 945–981.

Oman, D., & Neuhauser, L. (2012). Spiritual factors in occupational health and well-being: Opportunities for research translation. In P. C. Hill & B. J. Dik (Eds.), *Psychology of religion and workplace spirituality* (pp. 63–85). IAP Information Age.

Osunde, E., Tlou, J., & Brown, N. (1996). Persisting and common stereotypes in U. S. students' knowledge of Africa: A study of pervasive social studies teachers. *Social Studies*, 87, 119–124.

Bibliography 135

Pert, C. B. (1997). *Molecules of emotion: The science behind mind–body medicine.* Touchstone.

Piaget, J. (1974). *The language and thought of the child.* New American Library.

Pinxten, R. (2009). Universalism and relativism of knowledge dissipate: The intercultural perspective. In N. Note (Ed.), *Worldviews and cultures: Philosophical reflections from an intercultural perspective* (pp. 191–200). Springer.

Popper, K. (1959). *The logic of scientific discovery.* Hutchinson.

Potter, J. (1996). *Representing reality.* Sage.

Potter, J. (1997). Discourse analysis as a way of analyzing naturally occurring talk. In D. Silverman (Ed.), *Qualitative research.* Sage.

Powell, M. L., & Newgent, R. A. (2010). Improving the empirical credibility of cinematherapy: A single-subject interrupted time-series design. *Counseling Outcome Research and Evaluation, 1*(2), 40–49.

Raingruber, B. (2003). Integrating aesthetics into advanced practice mental health nursing: Commercial film as suggested modality. *Issues in Mental Health Nursing, 24,* 467–495.

Razee, S. (Ed.). (1993). *Najolbalaghe of Imam Alil (Alayhessalam).* Hejrat Publications.

Reinharz, S. (1992). *Feminist methods in social science research.* Oxford University Press.

Richards, I. A. (1923). *The meaning of meaning.* Harcourt, Brace & World.

Richards, R. (Ed.). (2007). *Everyday creativity and new views of human nature: Psychological, social and spiritual perspectives.* American Psychological Association.

Ricoeur, P. (1970). *Freud and philosophy.* Yale University Press.

Ricoeur, P. (1976). *Interpretation theory: Discourse and the surplus of meaning.* Texas University Press.

Ricoeur, P. (1978). *The philosophy of Paul Ricoeur.* Duquesne University Press.

Ricoeur, P. (1981). *Hermeneutics and the human sciences.* Cambridge University Press.

Ricoeur, P. (1991a). *From text to action: Essays in hermeneutics.* Northwestern University Press.

Ricoeur, P. (1991b). *A Ricoeur reader; reflection and imagination.* University of Toronto Press.

Ricoeur, P. (1998). *Critique and conviction.* Polity.

Rosenhan, D., & Seligman, M. E. P. (1995). *Abnormal psychology.* W. W. Norton.

Sabbadini, A. (2014). *Moving images.* Routledge.

Sa'di, S. M. (1998). *Koleyyate Sa'di.* Forooghi.

Said, E. W. (1978). *Orientalism.* Random House.

Said, E. W. (1993). *Culture and imperialism.* Alfred A. Knopf.

Said, E. W. (1997). *Covering Islam.* Vintage.

Schnall, S., & Roper, J. (2011). Elevation puts moral values into action. *Social Psychological and Personality Science, 3*(3), 373–378. doi:10.1177/1948550611423595.

Schneider, F. W., Gruman, J. A., & Coutts, L. M. (2012). *Applied social psychology: Understanding and addressing social and practical problems.* Oxford University Press.

Schneider, K. (1998). Toward a science of the heart: Romanticism and the revival of psychology. *American Psychologist, 53,* 277–298.

Schneider, K. (2011). Awakening to an awe-based psychology. *The Humanistic Psychologist, 39,* 247–252.

Schneider, K. (2013). *The polarized mind: Why it's killing us and what we can do about it.* University Professors Press.

136 Bibliography

Schneider, K. (2018). The chief peril is not a DSM diagnosis but the polarized mind. *Journal of Humanistic Psychology*, 59, 99–106.

Schneider, K., & Fatemi, S. M. (2019). Polarized mind. *Scientific American*. https://blogs.scientificamerican.com/observations/todays-biggest-threat-thepolarizedmind/?previewid=.

Schulenberg, S. (2003). Psychotherapy and movies: On using films in clinical practice. *Journal of Contemporary Psychotherapy*, 33, 35–48.

Schulz, R. (1976). Effects of control and predictability on the physical and psychological well-being of the institutionalized aged. *Journal of Personality and Social Psychology*, 33, 563–573.

Schulz, R., & Brenner, G. (1977). Relocation of the aged: A review and theoretical analysis. *Journal of Gerontology*, 3, 323–333.

Schulz, R., & Hanusa, B. H. (1978). Long-term effects of predictability and control enhancing interventions: Findings and ethical issues. *Journal of Personality and Social Psychology*, 36, 1194–1201.

Schulz, R., & Hanusa, B. H. (1979). *Environmental influences on the effectiveness of control and competence enhancing interventions*. In L. C. Perlmuter & R. A. Monty (Eds.), *Choice and perceived control* (pp. 315–337). Erlbaum.

Schulz, R., & Heckhausen, J. (1996). A life span model of successful aging. *American Psychologist*, 51, 702–714.

Schulz, R., & Heckhausen, J. (1997). Emotions and control: A life span perspective. In M. P. Lawton & K. W. Schaie (Eds.), *Annual review of gerontology and geriatrics* (Vol. 17, pp. 185–205). Springer.

Schulz, R., Heckhausen, J., & Locher, J. (1991). Adult development, control, and adaptive functioning. *Journal of Social Issues*, 47, 177–196.

Schulz, R., Wrosch, C., Yee, J. L., & Heckhausen, J. (1999). *Control strategies moderate the relations between physical illness and depression*. Manuscript submitted for publication.

Scileppi, J. A., Teed, E. L., & Torres, R. D. (2000). *Community psychology, a common sense approach to mental health*. Prentice-Hall.

Scruton, R. (2009). Confronting biology. In C. S. Titus (Ed.), *Philosophical psychology: Psychology, emotion and freedom* (pp. 68–107). The Institute for the Psychological Sciences Press.

Shariati, A. (1998). *Hajj* (L. Bakhtian, Trans.). Islamic Publications International.

Shotter, J. (1993). *Conversational realities*. Sage.

Silverman, K. (1983). *The subject of semiotics*. Oxford University Press.

Silvers, J., & Haidt, J. (2008). Moral elevation can induce nursing. *Emotion*, 8(2), 291–295. https://doi.org/10.1037/1528-3542.8.2.291.

Slife, B. D., & Gnatt, E. E. (1999). Methodological pluralism: A framework for psychotherapy research. *Journal of Clinical Psychology*, 55, 1453–1465.

Snyder, I. (Ed.). (2002). *Silicon literacies. Communication, innovation and education in the electronic age*. Routledge.

Spariosu, M. I. (2004). *Global intelligence and human development: Toward an ecology of global learning*. The MIT Press.

Stein, J., Salomon, G., & McDonald, D. (1979). Educational media. *Communication Booknotes*, 11(3), 79–81. doi:10.1080/10948007909488739.

Stephens, J. M., & Gehlbach, H. (2006). Under pressure and under-engaged: Motivational profiles and academic cheating in high school. In E. Anderman and T. Murdock (Eds.), *The psychology of academic cheating*. Elsevier.

Bibliography 137

Sternberg, R. J. (1985). *Beyond IQ: A triarchic theory of human intelligence.* Cambridge University Press.

Sternberg, R. J. (1988a). A three-facet model of creativity. In R. Sternberg (Ed.), *The nature of creativity* (pp. 125–147). Cambridge University Press.

Sternberg, R. J. (1988b). *The triangle of love: Intimacy, passion, commitment.* Basic Books.

Sternberg, R. J. (Ed.). (1990). *Wisdom: Its nature, origins, and development.* Cambridge University Press.

Sternberg, R. J. (1997a). *Successful intelligence.* Plume.

Sternberg, R. J. (1997b). *Thinking styles.* Cambridge University Press.

Sternberg, R. J. (1998). A balance theory of wisdom. *Review of General Psychology, 2,* 347–365.

Sternberg, R. J. (2001). Why schools should teach for wisdom: The balance theory of wisdom in educational settings. *Educational Psychologist, 36,* 227–245.

Sternberg, R. J. (2002). *Why smart people can be so stupid.* Yale University Press.

Sternberg, R. J. (2006). A duplex theory of love. In R. J. Sternberg & K. Weis (Eds.), *The new psychology of love* (pp. 184–199). Yale University Press.

Sternberg, R. J., & Davidson, J. (1985). Competence and performance in intellectual development. In E. D. Neimark, R. D. List, & J. L. Newman (Eds.), *Moderators of performance* (pp. 79–96). Lawrence Erlbaum.

Stubbs, M. (1983). *Discourse analysis: The sociolinguistic analysis of natural language.* University of Chicago Press.

Sue, S., & Zane, N. (1995). The role of culture and cultural techniques in psychotherapy: A critique and reformulation. In N. R. Goldberger & J. B. Veroff (Eds.), *The culture and psychology reader* (pp. 767–788). New York University Press.

Sullivan, P., & Feltz, D. (2003). The preliminary development of the Scale for Effective Communication in Team Sports (SECTS). *Journal of Applied Social Psychology, 33*(8), 1693–1715. doi:10.1111/j.1559-1816.2003.tb01970.x.

Sundararajan, L. (2005). Happiness donut: A Confucian critique of positive psychology. *Journal of Theoretical and Philosophical Psychology, 25,* 35–60.

Swanger, D. (1990). *Essays in aesthetic education.* Edwin Meller Press.

Sweeney, P. J., & Fry, L. W. (2012). Character development through spiritual leadership. *Consulting Psychology Journal: Practice and Research, 64*(2), 89–107.

Syversten, A. K., & Flanagan, C. A. (2005). *CYF news.* American Psychological Association.

Tacey, D. (2007). *How to read Jung.* W. W. Norton & Co.

Takkinen, S., Suutama, T., & Ruoppila, I. (2001). More meaning by exercising? Physical activity as a predictor of a sense of meaning in life and of self-rated health and functioning in old age. *Journal of Aging and Physical Activity, 9,* 128–141.

Tan, E. S.-H. (2018). A psychology of the film. *Palgrave Communications, 4*(1). doi:10.1057/s41599-018-0111-y.

Tan, E. S.-H., & Visch, V. (2018). Co-imagination of fictional worlds in film viewing. *Review of General Psychology, 22*(2), 230–244. doi:10.1037/gpr0000153.

Tangney, J. P. (2000). Humility: Theoretical perspectives, empirical findings and directions for future research. *Journal of Social & Clinical Psychology, 19,* 70–82.

Teo, T. (2005). *The critique of psychology: From Kant to postcolonial theory.* Springer.

138 *Bibliography*

Titus, C. S. (Ed.). (2009). *Philosophical psychology: Psychology, emotions, and freedom.* Institute for the Psychological Sciences Press.

Tolman, C. W. (1994). *Psychology, society, and subjectivity: An introduction to German critical psychology.* Routledge.

Toman, S., & Rak, C. (2000). The use of cinema in the counselor education curriculum: Strategies and outcome. *Counselor Education and Supervision, 40,* 105–114.

Tucker, J. L. (2009). *Visions in global education: The globalization of curriculum and pedagogy in teacher education and schools: Perspectives from Canada, Russia, and the United States.* Peter Lang.

Turner, B. S. (1993). Contemporary problems in the theory of citizenship. In B. S. Turner (Ed.), *Citizenship and social theory* (pp. 1–18). Sage.

Ussher, A. (1955). *Journey through dread.* Devin-Adair.

Vaillant, G. E. (2004). Positive aging. In P. A. Linely & S. Joseph (Eds.), *Positive psychology in practice.* John Wiley & Sons.

Vaillant, G. E. (2008). *Spiritual evolution: A scientific defence of faith.* Broadway Books.

Van Lier, L. (2000). From input to affordance: Social-interactive learning from an ecological perspective. In J. P. Lantolf (Ed.), *Sociocultural theory and second language learning* (pp. 245–259). Oxford University Press.

Vandrick, S. (1994). Feminist pedagogy and ESL. *College ESL, 4*(2), 69–92.

Vanm-maanen, J. (1979). The fact or fiction in organizational ethnography. *Administrative Science Quarterly, 24,* 539–550.

Volosinov, V. (1973). *Marxism and the philosophy of language.* Seminar Press.

Vygotsky, L. S. (1962). *Thought and language.* MIT Press.

Walsh-Bowers, R. W. (2005). Expanding the terrain of constructing the subject. In M. C. Chung (Ed.), *Rediscovering the history of psychology: Essays inspired by the work of Kurt Danziger* (pp. 97–118). Kluwer Academic.

Waugh, L. (1976). *Roman Jackobson's science of language.* The Peter DE Ridder Press.

Wedding, D., Boyd, M. A., & Niemiec, R. M. (2010). *Movies and mental illness: Using films to understand psychopathology* (3rd ed.). Hogrefe.

Wedding, D., & Niemiec, R. M. (2003). The clinical use of films in psychotherapy. *Journal of Clinical Psychology, 59*(2), 207–216.

Wedding, D., & Niemiec, R. M. (2014). *Movies and mental illness: Using films to understand psychopathology* (4th ed.). Hogrefe.

Weinstein, N., & Ryan, R. (2010). When helping helps: Autonomous motivation for pro-social behavior and its influence on well-being for the helper and recipient. *Journal of Personality and Social Psychology, 98*(2), 222–244.

Werner, H. (1955). *On expressive language.* Clark University Press.

Whaley, D. L., & Surratt, S. L. (1967). *Attitudes of science* (3rd ed.). Behaviordelia.

Weinstein, N., & Ryan, R. (2010). When helping helps: Autonomous motivation for pro-social behavior and its influence on well-being for the helper and recipient. *Journal of Personality and Social Psychology, 98*(2), 222–244.

Whiston, S. (2000). *Principles and applications of assessment in counseling.* Brooks/Cole.

White, D. A. (1978). *Heidegger and the language of poetry.* University of Nebraska.

Widmeyer, W., & Williams, J. (1991). Predicting cohesion in a coacting sport. *Small Group Research, 22*(4), 548–570. doi:10.1177/1046496491224007.

Willinsky, J. (1998). *Learning to divide the world: Education at empire's end.* University of Minnesota Press.

Winston, A. (2001). Cause into function: Ernst Mach and the reconstruction of explanation in psychology. In C. D. Green, M. Shore, & T. Teo (Eds.), *The transformation of psychology: Influences of 19th-century philosophy, technology, and natural science* (pp. 107–131). American Psychological Association. doi:10.1037/10416-006.

Wittgenstein, L. (1963). *Philosophical investigations* (G. Anscombe, Trans.). Macmillan.

Wittgenstein, L. (1968). *Philosophical investigations* (3rd ed.). (G. E. M. Anscombe, Trans.). Basil Blackwell. (Original work published 1953)

Wittgenstein, L. (1974). *Philosophical grammar* (A. Kenny, Trans.). Basil Blackwell.

Zajonc, R. B. (1984). On the primacy of affect. *American Psychologist*, 39, 117–123.

Zenner, C., Herrnleben-Kurz, S., & Walatch, H. (2014). Mindfulness-based interventions in schools—A systematic review and meta-analysis. *Frontiers in Psychology*, 5, 603.

Ziman, J. M. (1991). *Reliable knowledge: An exploration of the grounds for belief in science.* Cambridge University Press.

Zoogman, S., Goldberg, S., Hoyt, W., & Miller, L. (2014). Mindfulness interventions with youth: A meta-analysis. *Mindfulness*, 6(2), 1–13.

Index

Note: Page references in *italic* refer to figures

12 Angry Men (1957) 31, 33, 34
abuse 4
Adventures of Robinhood, The (1938) 70
affairs 5
Ali's Wedding (2017) 68, 90
All the President's Men (1976) 95
Amelie (2001) 50
American Dreams (2006) 50
American in Paris, An (1951) 38
American Psycho (2002) 47, 111
Analyze This (1999) 5
Annie Hall (1977) 5
anxiety 3, 5, 11, 26
Apartment, The (1960) 33
Apocalypse Now (1979) 36
apparatus theory 14
As It Is in Heaven (2004) 50
authority 101, 102, 104
Awakening, The (1980) 90
Awakenings (1990) 32
Away From Her (2006) 76

Back to the Future (1990) 70
Bajrangi Bhaijaan (2015) 50, 54
Baruch, R. 2
Basketball Diaries, The (1995) 114
Batman Begins (2005) 24
Baudry, J.-L. 14
Bean (1997) 46
Beautiful Mind, A (2001) 4, 5, 6, 35–36
Beauty and the Beast (1991) 68
Beauty and the Beast (2017) 88
Bedeviled (2016) 4
Before Midnight (2013) 4
behavior 1, 3, 11, 12, 21, 47, 91; *see also* emotions

Bellah, R. et al. 82
Beowulf (2007) 115
Berg-Cross, L. 2
Better Life, A (2011) 93
Bicycle Thief (1948) 92
Big Miracle (2012) 5
Birds, The (1963) 13
Black Swan (2010) 4, 12, 16
Blind Side, The (2009) 93
Blow (2001) 5
Blue Valentine (2010) 4
Born on the Fourth of July (1989) 5
Brain on Fire (2016) 30
Brassed Off (1996) 5
Braveheart (1995) 115
Breakdown (1955) 69
Breakfast Club, The (1985) 4
Bright Star (2009) 114
Britton, C. 13
Brown, N. 100
Bruner, J. 1, 82

Casablanca (1942) 36, 38–39
Casbah (1948) 31–32
Cast Away (2000) 50, 61, 90
Cathy Come Home (1966) 33, 96
Cat on a Hot Tin Roof (1958) 33
children 15, 49, 94, 99
Christmas Carol, A (1938) 50
Christmas Carol, A (1951) 67–68
Christmas Carol, A (2009) 27, 91
Cinderella (2015) 88
cinema therapy 2
Citizen Kane (1941) 12, 36, 37, 38, 40
Clockwork Orange, The (1971) 16
Close Encounters of the Third Kind (1977) 95

Index 141

Clueless (1995) 111
cognitive understanding 21, 26, 33, 49
colonialism 104–105
Coming Home (1978) 5
communication 4–5, 22, 23, 33, 40,
46–47, 48
Compulsion (1959) 36–37
consumerism 40–41, 92, 109,
110–111, 112
Contact (1997) 76, 92
control 5, 15, 19, 29, 64–65, 79
Crazy Love (2007) 33
creativity 18, 30, 32, 81–82, 84–85, 87,
119–120, 121–122, 123
Crum, A. J. 64

Dark Past, The (1948) 91
Da Vinci Code, The (2006) 91
Day After Tomorrow, The (2004) 33
Dead Poets Society (1989) 65,
114–115, 121
deconstructionism 7, 26–27, 30, 97, 101
Deer Hunter, The (1978) 5
depression 5, 25, 26
development 56–60
Dial M for Murder (1954) 44, 48, 72
dialogues 3, 4, 35–37, 40, 41, 42, 47–
48, 101
Dirty Harry (1971) 95
divorce 4
Domino Principle (1977) 95
Drive (2011) 47
Dr. Mobuse (1933) 16
Dr. Zhivago (1965) 91, 113
Dying to Dance (2001) 5

eating disorders 5
Eco, U. 75, 77
Eden (2016) 4
educational tool 1, 7, 35
ego 10–11
emotions 2–3, 21, 49, 61–63, 65–68,
72, 93
extralinguistic components 51, 52–53;
see also language
Extremely Loud and Incredibly Close
(2011) 5

Far and Away (1992) 5
feminist psychoanalytical theory 14
Fight Club (1999) 111
films 1–9, 15, 81, 95–96, 110
film theory 10, 14
film therapy 89–94

Fish Tank (2009) 61
Flight (2012) 5
Forrest Gump (1994) 6, 37, *38*, 65, 91
For the Love of Nancy (1994) 5
Founder, The (2016) 5
Freeway II: Confessions of a Trickbaby
(1999) 5
Freidrich, P. 118
Freire, P. 105
French Connection, The (1975) 95–96
Friends (2011) 24

Gandhi (1982) 4, 50, 60
Gibbs, R. W. 118
Gills 106
Girl, Interrupted (1999) 4, 5
Glengarry Glen Ross (1992) 40–41,
89–90, 91, 111
global citizenship 105, 106, 107, 108
global education 96, 97–102, 104,
105–106, 107–109
globalization 96, 97, 105, 106–107
global wisdom 72, 109
goals 4–6, 24, 102
Godfather, The (1972) 36, 70
Gone With the Wind (1939) 36
Good Will Hunting (1997) 4
Graduate, The (1967) 46, *47*
Gran Torino (2008) 65
Grapes of Wrath, The (1940) 17
grief 5
Guess Who's Coming to Dinner (1967)
7, 18, 31, 33, 48

Hacksaw Ridge (2016) 30–31, 40, 68, 91
Ha'iri Yazdi, M. 83
Hakimi, M. R. 103, 107
Harvey (1950) 93
Heat of the Night (1967) 65–66
Hellen Keller (1920) 36
Herda, E. A. 79
High Anxiety (1977) 5
High School Musical (2008) 24
Hospital, The (2013) 5
Hotel Rwanda (2004) 92
Hours, The (2002) 5
Howl (2015) 114, 121
Hubble et al. 86
Huntington 101, 102, 103, 107
Hurricane, The (1999) 6, 60, 113

I Am a Fugitive From a Chain Gang
(1932) 32, 38, *39*, 60, 71, 91, *92*, 113
I Confess (1953) 11, 32, *56*, 57

142 Index

id 10, 11
Ideal Husband, An (1947) 4
identification 14, 19
imaginary 14, 15
In Country (1989) 5
Inside Out (2015) 61
intralinguistic components 51–52; *see also* language
Iris (2001) 76
Iron Man (2008) 5
Islamic worldview 99, 102–103, 107
It Is Complicated (2009) 4
It's a Wonderful Life (1946) 5

Jafari, M. T. 102–103, 107
James, W. 29
Jennings, P. 2
J.F.K. (1991) 113
Johnston, J. 77–78
Jung, C. G. 80–82, 83–84, 85, 86–87

Kant, I. 117
Karate Kid, The (2010) 69, 71
Kid, The (2019) 93
Kierkegaard, S. 69
knowledge 64, 72, 80–81, 82, 83, 105; *see also* global education; wisdom
Kramer vs. Kramer (1979) 4, 17, 33

Lacan, J. 10, 15
Lacanian psychoanalysis 10, 14–15, 49
Langer, E. J. 20–21, 24, 28, 63, 64, 101
Langerian mindfulness 17, 19, 20, 21, 23, 24, 25, 26–27, 28, 29–30, 63, 64
language 15, 25, 51, 83, 85–86, 91, 117–118, 120–121; creativity 119–120, 121–122; mindfulness 25, 30–31; poetry 115–117, 118–119, 120; understanding 81, 82
Lasn, K. 84
Last Emperor, The (1987) 5
Last King of Scotland, The (2006) 5
Latour, B. 109–110
Lawrence of Arabia (1962) 91
Lean on Me (1989) 6–7
learning 1, 2, 7, 20, 79; *see also* global education
Les Misérables (1998) 69, 73
Les Misérables (2012) 91, 92, 113
Lewis, Bernard 107
Life Is Beautiful (1997) 50
Life of Emile Zola, The (1937) 53, *112*, 113
Life of Pi (2012) 5, 50, 92, *93*

Lincoln (2012) 4
linguistic systems 51–53, 118, 119; *see also* language
Lion (2016) 90
Lion King, The (2019) 37, 91
Lion of the Desert (1981) 91
Little Children (2006) 5
Little Miss Sunshine (2006) 5
Lost in Translation (2003) 5, 32, 90
Love in the Afternoon (1957) 36
Love Story (1970) 36
Lucy (2014) 50
Lyddy, C. 64

Macbeth (2015) 5
McDonald, D. 2
Madam X (1994) 33
Mad Love (1995) 5
Man for All Seasons, A (1966) 4
Marnie (1964) 11, 12, 15–16, 91
Martin Luther (1953) 5
materialism 40–41, 92, 102, 106, 109, 110–111
Matrix, The (1999) 50
meanings 4–5, 7, 12, 14, 32, 35, 50, 90; *see also* verbal components; visual components; vocal components
mental challenges 4
mental disorders 5
Merryfield, M. M. 101–102
Message, The (1976) 60
Metz, C. 13, 14
Midnight in Paris (2011) 32, 91
Miles, S. 111
mindfulness 17–22, 23, 24, 25–28, 29–34, 63, 64, 91
mindlessness 17, 18, 19–21, 23–24, 25, 26, 29, 30, 91, 101
Miracles From Heaven (2016) 5
Miracle Worker, The (1962) 28, 59
mirror stage 14–15
Modern Romance (2017) 33
Modern Times (1936) 46
Mona Lisa Smile (2003) 57
Moonlight (2016) 61
Morgan, B. 85
movies *see* films
Mr. Jones (2019) 5
Mr. Nobody (2009) 50
Mrs. Doubtfire (1993) 4
Mr. Smith Goes to Washington (1939) 4
Muhammad: The Messenger of God (1976) 5
Mulan (2020) 115

Index 143

Mulvey, L. 10, 14
Münsterberg, H. 10
music 38
My Big Fat Greek Wedding (2002) 90
My Fair Lady (1964) 6, 30–31
My Family (1995) 5
Mystic River (2003) 5

Nafas (2016) 69
narratives 12, 31, 49, 51, 52–53, 82, 85, 94, 120
negative emotions 2, 25, 30, 62
Niemiec, R. M. 1, 62
Nightmare Before Christmas, The (2020) 114
Night on Earth (1991) 25, 32, 33, 43–44, 96–97
Nixon (1995) 113
North by Northwest (1959) 47
Notebook, The (2004) 4, 91
Notes on a Scandal (2006) 5

Oakeshott, M. 78–79
O Brother, Where Art Thou? (2000) 114, 122–123
observation 3, 7, 15
October Sky (1999) 65
On Golden Pond (1981) 93
Osunde, E. 100
ownership 101, 102, 104
Oxford rowing crew (boat race, 1987) 22–23, 24

Papillon (1973) 6
Parallax View, The (1974) 95
Parent Trap, The (1998) 4
Party (1968) 25
Patch of Blue (1965) 18
Paterson (2016) 114
Perfect Body (1997) 5
performance 24, 62–63
Perks of Being a Wallflower (2012) 6
personality 10–11
perspectives 17–18, 25, 31, 33, 91
Phantom of the Opera (1989) 90
phenomenology 19, 31, 64, 72
physical challenges 4
Pian, The (1993) 5
Place in the Sun, A (1951) 68
Planck, M. 72
poetry 114, 115–117, 118–119, 120, 121–122, 123
Poetry (2010) 114
political issues 95–97, 111, 113

Portrait of Jennie, The (1948) 76
positive emotions 1, 2, 24, 45–46, 62, 93
possibilities 22, 24, 25, 26, 28, 29
posttraumatic stress disorder 5
power 5, 101, 104, 105, 106–107
President, The (2014) 113
Pretty Woman (1990) 110–111
Pride and Prejudice (2005) 51
Prince and The Pauper (1937) 31, 91
P.S. I Love You (2007) 5
Psycho (1960) 12, 15–16, 38
psychoanalysis 10–16
psychoanalytic theory 10–11, 14–15
psychological perspectives 90, 109–110
Pursuit of Happyness, The (2006) 70–71

Rain Man (1988) 4
Raven, The (2012) 115
Reader, The (2008) 61
referent 75, 77
relationships 4, 33, 43–48, 58, 94
religion 5
Repulsion (1965) 16
Requiem for a Dream (2000) 61
Revolutionary Road (2008) 46
Richards, I. A. 116
Ricoeur, P. 81, 85–86, 115, 118–120
Robinhood (2018) 19
Rocky (1976) 95, *96*
Rodin, J. 63, 64
Romeo and Juliet (Shakespeare) 58
Rosetta (1999) 33, 96

Said, E. W. 104–105, 107–108
Salomon, G. 2
Saving Private Ryan (1998) 5
Scarlet Street (1945) 32, 44–45, 66–67, 91
Scenes From a Marriage (1974) 33
Scent of a Woman (1992) 36, 91
Schulz, R. 63–64
Science of Sleep (2006) 16
Secret Between Friends, A (1996) 5
Secrets of a Soul (1926) 13
Selma (2014) 33, 96
Separation, A (2011) 33
Seven Year Itch, The (1955) 5
Shadow of a Doubt (1943) 13
Shakespeare in Love (1998) 115
Shame (2011) 16
Sharing the Secret (2000) 5
Shawshank Redemption, The (1994) 6, 38, 75–76
Shotter, J. 78
Showgirls (1995) 78

144   Index

significations 75–76, 77, 78, 84, 88
signified 75, 77, 88, 99–100
signifiers 75, 77, 88, 99–100
signs 75–80, 82, 83, 84–85, 86, 87, 88, 99–100
Silence (2016) 30, 48
Silver Linings Playbook (2012) 4, 5
Snyder, I. 79
social awareness 95, 96, 98, 112–113
Song of Bernadette, The (1943) 58
Sound of Music, The (1965) 30–31, 90, 123
Space Odyssey, A (1968) 70
Spariosu, M. I. 98, 100–101, 103, 104, 106–107
spirituality 57, 92
Splendor in the Grass (1961) 47, 122
Split (2016) 16
Spring, Summer, Fall, Winter … and Spring (2003) 50
Star Wars (2017) 95
Stein, J. 2
Sternberg, R. J. 70
Still Alice (2014) 4
Striptease (1996) 78
Student of Prague, The (1913) 16
substance disorders 5
Sudden Impact (1983) 36
Sunset Boulevard (1950) 25
super ego 11
Superman (1987) 95
Super Size Me (2004) 65, 96
Swanger, D. 116
Sylvia (1965) 115
Sylvia Plath (2003) 115
symbolic order 15
symbols 75, 76–77, 80, 81–82, 83–84, 85, 86–87, 88

Tacey, D 80, 81, 85
Taxi Driver (1976) 36
Teo, T. 110
text, films as 3–4, 75, 82, 89, 90
therapeutic tool 1, 2, 3–6, 7–9, 89–94
thinking styles 1, 23, 28, 33, 62, 80–81, 109
Thirteen Days (2000) 4
Titanic (1997) 2–3, 70, 91
Tlou, J. 100

To Kill a Mockingbird (1962) *33*, 89
tolerance 5
Tom & Viv (1994) 115
To the Bone (2017) 5
Troy (2004) 115
Truly Madly Deeply (1990) 5
Tuesdays With Morrie (1999) 69, 71

unconscious components 11, 12, 91
understanding 21, 26, 33, 49–55, 71–72, 81, 82, 90
Under the Tuscan Sun (2003) 4
Unfaithful (2002) 5
Unsane (2018) 68
utilitarianism 40–41, 78, 79, 85, 90, 92, 98, 102, 110

Vaillant, G. E. 57
values 1, 4, 57, 70
verbal components 35–37, 41, 42, 47–48
Vice (2018) 60
violence 102, 108
visual components 39–41, 47
vocal components 37–39, 41, 47
von Herder, J. G. 117

Walk to Remember, A (2002) 91
Wall Street (1987) 5
War of the Roses, The (1989) 33
Way We Were, The (1973) 33
Wedding, D. 1, 62
well-being 41, 47, 69
Wells, O. 114
We're No Angels (1955) 92
We're No Angels (1989) 44
Who's Afraid of Virginia Woolf (1966) 33, 46, 48
Wings of Desire (1987) 61
Winter Kills (1979) 95
wisdom 69–74, 109
Wittgenstein, L. 50, 118
Wizard of Oz, The (1939) 36, 88
Wolf of Wall Street, The (2013) 30–31, 56–57, 90, 91, 113
Wrong Man, The (1956) 57, 60, 92

Young Adult (2011) 5

Zapata (1970) 19

Printed in the United States
by Baker & Taylor Publisher Services